Pat Jones'
Tales from Oklahoma State Football

PAT JONES
WITH JIMMIE TRAMEL

SportsPublishingLLC.com

ISBN-13: 978-1-59670-211-0

© 2007 by Pat Jones and Jimmie Tramel

All rights reserved. Except for use in a review, the reproduction or utilization of this work in any form or by any electronic, mechanical, or other means, now known or hereafter invented, including xerography, photocopying, and recording, and in any information storage and retrieval system, is forbidden without the written permission of the publisher.

Publishers: Peter L. Bannon and Joseph J. Bannon Sr.
Senior managing editor: Susan M. Moyer
Developmental editor: Laura E. Podeschi
Art director: Dustin J. Hubbart
Cover design: Dustin J. Hubbart
Interior design: Kathryn R. Holleman

Sports Publishing L.L.C.
804 North Neil Street
Champaign, IL 61820
Phone: 1-877-424-2665
Fax: 217-363-2073
www.SportsPublishingLLC.com

Printed in the United States of America

CIP data available upon request.

Contents

PROLOGUE v

Chapter One
NEW SHERIFF IN TOWN 1

Chapter Two
SETTING THE TONE 7

Chapter Three
KNOCKING THEIR EYES OUT 21

Chapter Four
GOING BOWLING 28

Chapter Five
ERNEST LEADS THE NATION 35

Chapter Six
BATTLING THE BIG RED MACHINE 45

Chapter Seven
GOODBYE JIMMY, HELLO MR. IBA 64

Chapter Eight
RUN FOR THE NATIONAL TITLE 72

Chapter Nine
THURMAN BREAKS THROUGH 91

Chapter Ten
GOING WITH GUNDY 114

Chapter Eleven
   CHRISTMAS IN EL PASO 129

Chapter Twelve
   RUN TO THE HEISMAN 147

Chapter Thirteen
   FINAL THOUGHTS 174

INDEX 180

Prologue

People who read this book are going to get a taste of lightning in a bottle.

Let me explain what I mean by that. Flash back to September 8, 1984. Oklahoma State went on the road in my head coaching debut and smashed an Arizona State team that one preseason magazine picked to win the national championship.

We went to the Phoenix airport after the game, and we were all buzzing with excitement. I overheard our sports information director, Pat Quinn, say this to the *Tulsa World*'s sports editor, Bill Connors: "Bill, it looks like this team has caught lightning in a bottle."

That statement summed up how I feel about my first decade at Oklahoma State, including the five years spent as an assistant to Jimmy Johnson and my first five years as head coach.

We did catch lightning in a bottle, and I think you will agree with me that it was one of the most exciting periods in the history of OSU football. We had three 10-win seasons. We placed lower than third in the Big Eight only twice. We played in six bowl games. We competed for high stakes and were essentially in a two-game playoff for the national championship in 1984.

That era of Cowboy football featured All-Americans like John Corker, Ricky Young, Gary Lewis, Larry Roach, Ernest Anderson, Rod Brown, Hart Lee Dykes, Leslie O'Neal, Mark Moore, Thurman Thomas, and Barry Sanders, who won the Heisman Trophy in 1988 and helped us lead the nation in scoring.

I want to thank all the Oklahoma State players and coaches for the efforts they put in during my 16 years in Stillwater. This book chronicles 10 of those years, concluding with Sanders' run to the Heisman Trophy.

Both Jimmie Tramel, who partnered with me on this book, and I would also like to thank all the people who made this project possible, including the late Bill Connors, who was a dear friend for many years.

To all you loyal Oklahoma State fans and to football fans across the great state of Oklahoma, I hope you enjoy my remembrances of these 10 years as much as I enjoyed living through them.

—PAT JONES,
OSU head football coach, 1984-1994

CHAPTER 1

New Sheriff in Town

HOW 'BOUT THEM COWBOYS?

Let's start this book with a revelation. It's common knowledge that Jerry Jones hired Jimmy Johnson to coach the Dallas Cowboys in 1989. But that was not the first time Jerry helped Jimmy get a job coaching a bunch of Cowboys.

After the 1978 college football season, Jerry played a role in helping Jimmy become head coach of the Oklahoma State Cowboys.

The relationship between Jerry and Jimmy goes way back. They played together at Arkansas, winning a national championship in 1964, and they were roommates on road trips. Their wives, Jean and Linda Kay, were sorority sisters.

After college, Jerry made a good bit of money in the oil and gas business. Jerry and one of his friends, Kevin Leonard, both had offices in the same Oklahoma City building.

Kevin was on the search committee when OSU was hiring a football coach to replace Jim Stanley. Because of the Jerry Jones-Kevin Leonard connection, Jimmy had an "in." Kevin prepped Jimmy very well as to who was on the search committee and what they might want to hear. And then, Jimmy being Jimmy, he made a big impression on the search committee because he was so upbeat and because Kevin had done a good job with him.

TAGGING ALONG

Obviously, the course of my life changed when Jimmy Johnson got the OSU job. He immediately hired me as an assistant coach and I became OSU's head coach five years later once Jimmy left for Miami.

When Jimmy began pursuing the Oklahoma State job, he and I were coaching together on Jackie Sherrill's staff at Pitt. We were at Taylor's, a bar in an upscale section of Pittsburgh, when he first told me he was going to interview at OSU. He asked me if I wanted to go with him if he got the job and asked me if I was ready to coach the defense. I answered "yes" to both questions.

I first met Jimmy when I was a college student. I transferred from Arkansas Tech to Arkansas and Jimmy was a graduate assistant on the Arkansas staff, but we really had no relationship at that time. Jimmy left and built a resume by paying dues at a high school in Picayune, Mississippi, and at colleges like Louisiana Tech, Wichita State, Iowa State, and Oklahoma.

Eventually, Jimmy returned to Arkansas, and by that time I was coaching high school ball in Little Rock. We had a great defensive lineman where I coached. That was one of the reasons why Arkansas hired me. There were really no staff limits at the time, and I helped Jimmy coach the defensive linemen.

I knew Jimmy had his act together already, but once we really got close, I knew he was a special guy. I wasn't the worldliest sort at all, but I knew he was going places.

THE COMPETITION

Who was chasing the OSU job when Jimmy got hired?

Joe Morrison, who would later become South Carolina's head coach, was a candidate. So was Leon Fuller, the defensive coordinator at Texas. Hayden Fry, the head coach at North Texas

State, probably could have had the job if he wanted it, but he went to Iowa. One night Jimmy called me and said, "Guess who else is trying to get this job?" Jimmy did not sound good. He was not very optimistic during that conversation, and he's obviously an optimistic person. The person who had him concerned was Grant Teaff. Jimmy felt like he had an upper hand as far as the other guys, but Teaff was a different entity because he was an established head coach at Baylor and had pulled off that "Miracle on the Brazos" when he took the Bears to the Cotton Bowl.

Jimmy was the last one brought in and he did such a great job in the interview session that I think they apparently huddled up right then and told him to stick around an extra day. He called me and said he was going to have to go out and buy some more clothes because he hadn't packed enough to stay another day. But they wanted to make an offer before he could go back to Pittsburgh. He called me later and said, "I've got this thing. We're going."

SERVING TWO MASTERS

It was immediately announced that two Pitt assistants, Tony Wise and I, would follow Jimmy to Stillwater. All of us, including Jimmy, told Jackie Sherrill we would stay on board at Pitt through the Tangerine Bowl that season. In hindsight, I think that taught us all a lesson that, if you can, you need to get on down the road in such situations.

During the course of our bowl week, Jimmy was trying to convince two other Pitt assistants, Larry Holton and Dave Wannstedt, to go to Stillwater. Well, Jackie was trying to convince them to stay, so that got a bit sticky. We ended up having separate staff meetings down there with the guys who were leaving and the guys who were staying. It was really a little bit tense.

We lost the bowl game and the week ended this way: As Jimmy and I changed clothes in the dressing room, one of the

This is Jimmy Johnson's first varsity staff at Oklahoma State in 1979, when he was the Big Eight's Coach of the Year. In the back row, Jimmy is surrounded by (left to right) Barry Pearson, Dave Wannstedt, Bob Leahy, and Paul Jette. In the front row are Larry Holton, Pat Jones, Tony Wise, and Jim Helms. *Photo courtesy of Oklahoma State University*

Pitt equipment men was ordered to stand next to us to make sure we didn't swipe any gear.

PUTTING THE BAND TOGETHER

Jimmy assembled a staff that ended up being a who's who of coaching. Take a look at that first staff picture, and it's mostly a group of upwardly mobile guys.

I became a head coach. Dave Wannstedt and Butch Davis, who started as our offensive graduate assistant, became college and NFL head coaches. Tony Wise has coached for many years in the NFL. We also hired Jim Helms, who had been a coach at OU and was the head coach at Cameron, along with Paul Jette, a former Texas defensive back. I think he was 24 years old at the time, but we needed a young recruiter. Larry Holton came from Pitt with us to coach the secondary. He has been a lot of places. Bill Miller, who was recently a defensive coordinator at Arizona State and some other big-time schools, became our defensive graduate assistant.

If I recall correctly, Jimmy was having a hard time hiring a veteran offensive coordinator. He wanted to appoint someone that knew the throwing game pretty well. Jimmy hired Bob Leahy, who had been a backup to Terry Bradshaw with the Steelers. Bob also had been a coordinator at Pitt and went to Cal after a conflict with Jackie Sherrill.

Bob had a little bit of a volatile personality (I'll have stories about this later), which Jimmy knew. But Jimmy kind of liked the guy. Jimmy appreciated Leahy's intellect. When Bob played for the Steelers, one of his teammates was Barry Pearson, who we hired as our receivers coach.

That was our staff. I'm sure someone else could have gotten the job done at Oklahoma State, but given the set of circumstances at that time, I'm not sure anyone could have done it much better.

MATCHING BARRY

Jimmy's energy and personality kick-started the Oklahoma State program. He was a human pep rally.

The coach before Jimmy, Jim Stanley, is a good man and was a very, very good football coach. We sensed early on that the players we inherited from him had been well coached. But Jim's personality and Jimmy's personality were just poles apart, especially in front of a camera. Hiring Jimmy helped OSU image-wise. You put OU coach Barry Switzer in front of a camera and you put Jimmy Johnson in front of a camera, and the game is on. I think from an image standpoint, Jimmy lit Stillwater up.

CHAPTER 2

Setting the Tone

1979

STATE OF THE UNION

Oklahoma State had won a share of the Big Eight title three seasons before we got there, but NCAA probation left us thin. We only had eight seniors and 62 scholarship players that first year.

We knew we didn't have much depth, but at the top of that roster were guys like Harold Bailey, Worley Taylor, Curtis Boone, Reggie Richardson, Dexter Manley, Steve Heinzler, Dean Prater, Gregg Johnson, Ricky Young, Pete DiClementi, Rick Antle, Doug Freeman, and John Corker. There were some talented guys, even if we didn't have many of them. We were not void of speed and quickness and we knew if we could stay reasonably healthy, we would be OK.

Harold Bailey, a senior quarterback, was a difference-maker for us physically and a heck of a guy. He was one of the greatest reclamation projects I have ever been around. He had only switched positions the year before, but Jimmy and Bob Leahy did a great job with him. At midseason, Jimmy campaigned for Harold to be named All-Big Eight quarterback. Harold didn't win it, but maybe he should have.

REUNITED WITH DEXTER

Dexter Manley was a junior when we arrived in Stillwater. Of course, Dexter would go on to be a great NFL defensive end, but his college career almost ended prematurely.

First, let me tell you about my initial meeting with Dexter. I was an assistant at SMU and I had gone with another coach, Steve Endicott, to see Dexter at Yates High School in Houston.

I remember telling Steve that if he wanted to recruit Manley, I would back him every step of the way because Manley was a talented guy. But I also had a bad feeling about this deal. Somebody was going to get in trouble for this thing. I'm not accusing anybody of anything, but all the warning signs were there. So we backed off him.

Lo and behold, when I get to OSU, Dexter is one of the first guys I see when I walk in the cafeteria. He sees me. He remembers me. He's such a likeable cuss anyway. He always just smiles and hugs you.

Years later, Oklahoma State was blamed, to put it mildly, when Manley spoke about his lack of reading ability. But the other part of the story was this: It seemed like virtually every morning in a staff meeting, somebody would come in to say we'd had a call from the campus police and Manley had done this or Manley had done that.

Finally, Jimmy told me maybe we ought to think about getting Dexter on down the road. And there are ways to do that. I said I would handle it.

Anyway, the first day we were allowed to be out with the players while they ran and did agility drills, Manley was impressive.

Outside linebacker/defensive end Dexter Manley was as gifted a pure athlete as any coach at OSU had ever seen. In 2002, he was selected as one of the top players in Washington Redskins history.
Photo courtesy of Oklahoma State University

I looked at Jimmy and Jimmy looked at me. We had already coached Hugh Green and Ricky Jackson, who were great players at Pitt. And Dexter was the best-looking guy you had ever seen. You couldn't touch him physically. I looked at Jimmy and I said, "Whoa, Coach, we've got to find a way to make this thing work." Jimmy was thinking the same thing. We were going to make it work. We had to see about this guy. He could blow up on us, but we had to find out what he was all about.

So we get started and Dexter lands in big-time trouble. He had filed forms that either his parents had passed away or he was divorced or something, and he had somehow received government money that he was ordered to repay. They are going to arrest him. It's a fed deal.

Manley needed help. He had an old car, so I talked to one of our buddies who was a car dealer. I said, "Look, whatever amount he owes the government, that's what this car is worth, OK? Buy the car from Dexter." It wasn't an illegal deal. The guy bought the car from Manley for whatever he owed the government. Then we had to get the check from Manley, which was not the easiest thing in the world to do. So we solved that. But it was a battle every single day with Manley, God bless him.

FIGHTING THE MONSTER

If you coach football at Oklahoma State, you have to cope with the shadow of that program down in Norman. Jimmy knew what was there because he had been an Oklahoma assistant. I knew what was there because I had dealt with them before. It's a monster—a huge entity. But on the same hand, you don't tell that to the rank and file.

Dr. Larry Boger, the OSU president who hired us, was a heck of a guy and liked to come to the stadium to watch practice. I remember him saying something like, "You can't worry about OU. You can't match them dollar for dollar, so you just take

Oklahoma State and make it the best you can." Which is kind of the approach we took.

MIAMI VICE

One of the players we inherited was John Corker, who had been a legitimate first-team All-American the year before. He tore his knee up toward the end of the previous season and he was still rehabbing when we got there, but he was unusually tall (about 6-foot-5) for an inside linebacker and, boy, what a gifted athlete!

John, who hailed from Miami, Florida, was always kind of on the fringe of one thing or another. At certain times, we wondered what John was getting into—or we didn't want to know.

We held him out of our first spring drills. He stayed around that summer, but went back to Miami two or three weeks before two-a-days. We really didn't want him to do that, but he did. By the time he came back, he had lost some ground with his knee. We were mad at him, so he picked up the pace again, took some hits, and continued to compete. We were protective of his injury, but we got a good year out of him.

Paul Jette coached John. Paul was 24 years old. John was probably 22. Paul had his hands full, but he did a good job. John was a vicious hitter and really a talented guy. He's still OSU's all-time leader in tackles.

AIR SHOW

In the first game of the Jimmy Johnson era, we beat North Texas 25-7, and Harold Bailey threw for 275 yards, fourth-most in school history. We knew North Texas was not a bad team because they had beaten OSU the year before and won nine games. We played well defensively, but trailed 7-6 going into the fourth quarter. North Texas was threatening to score again when Dexter Manley forced a fumble. Pete DiClementi recovered it, and we hit Ronald Ingram on a crossing route to break the game open.

That game itself was not our signature win, but was a big, emotional victory that set the tempo for the entire season.

THE SKYBIRD

We beat Wichita State 16-6 in our next game, but lost both starting outside linebackers, Dexter Manley and Rick Antle, to injuries.

Antle was a former walk-on and one of the toughest human beings I've ever been around. What was inside of Rick really defined what this group was all about. They were a bunch of gritty guys who refused to accept the fact that they weren't supposed to do what they were doing.

Antle had this thing he liked to call the "skybird," where he would jump over a blocker to get to the ball. That backfired against Wichita State. He tried to go above a blocking back and caught a helmet in the family jewels.

Afterward, I noticed Rick was not out there playing and asked about his status on the headphone. I was told he had cracked a nut. I thought they were talking about the nuts and bolts on a helmet, but they were talking about anatomy.

Rick was taken into the training room and his privates were purple and swollen up big. Supposedly, his father saw the damage and jokingly said, "Son, I've never been more proud of you than I am right now."

This will show you how tough Rick was. He told the doctor to take out a testicle immediately if it would get him on the field faster. That wasn't necessary. Rick was unable to return to that game, but he came back quicker than most guys would have.

Antle still makes people laugh when he tells the skybird story. But we weren't laughing when we tried to figure out how we would replace Manley and Antle against Arkansas the next week. We wanted to get our best available guys on the field, so rather than promote backups, we took players at other positions—Roger Taylor and Rodney Smith—and temporarily made them outside linebackers. They played fairly credibly, but we lost the game.

PARTY AT JERRY'S

The night before our game at Arkansas, our coaches attended a party at Jerry Jones' house. Jimmy was smart to continue to network with Jerry. Let me tell you why.

When Jerry was still pretty young, he tried to put an investment group together to buy the San Diego Chargers. It didn't happen. But Jimmy knew that, at some point in time, one of two things would happen: Jerry was going to buy a pro football team or Jimmy was going to have a shot at the Arkansas job, and Jerry could help him one way or another. We were over there to beat Arkansas, no question. But Jimmy is the smartest guy I have ever been around. His mind was working ahead.

ARRESTED DEVELOPMENT

I can't remember if this happened our first or second year at Oklahoma State—we made trips to Arkansas both seasons—but we were lucky to get out of Arkansas without one of our coaches being arrested.

Bob Leahy and I were always in the press box together because he called the offense and I called the defense. Bob was a volatile soul, to say the least. Any time a kid did anything wrong, whether causing a penalty or dropping a pass, it was a personal affront to Bob. And Bob was a banger and a hollerer and a yeller.

So we are in the press box at Arkansas when I look through a window and see that we are located next to the booth where the wives and children of the Arkansas staff are sitting. I know a bunch of them because I had coached at Arkansas. As the game begins, Bob is cutting loose with both barrels. Bob is pounding and hollering and cussing. I look over there next to us and people are grabbing their kids and walking out of the booth because of Bob.

Leaving the press box at halftime, I see a guy I went to high school with in Little Rock. It's Bo Marshall, who had worked his way up the ladder on the Little Rock police force. He tells me they have had so many complaints about Leahy that he would have to arrest him.

I pleaded with Bo not to do anything and said I would handle the situation. I told Bob to calm down because he was getting too wild, but my words probably went in one ear and out the other. After halftime, I had one of OSU's security people, Dan Martin, leave the field and stand at our press box door. We couldn't have one of our coaches arrested!

If the game had been over when Bo Marshall first talked to me, they might have taken Bob in. Fortunately, we knew Bo Marshall. It probably saved us from a real big incident.

CROWD CONTROL

We followed a loss at Arkansas with a 23-16 defeat at South Carolina. The Gamecocks had a running back, George Rogers, who won the Heisman the next season. Even though we lost, we left the game knowing we could play. We held up well on the road against a good team and validated ourselves a little.

The Leahy stuff spilled over on this trip. South Carolina had an open-air press box, which meant that the fans could hear him if he became loud. You could literally reach out and touch the fans' heads.

Anyway, Bob got into a back-and-forth exchange with them. Something would happen and Bob would say, "Take that!" or worse. It was a verbal sparring match between the Gamecock people and Bob. I remember telling Dave Wannstedt that I thought the fans were going to charge after us in the booth. And it was a close ballgame, so we didn't need any distractions.

I usually tried to get as far away from Bob as I could in the press box. I didn't like all the crazy stuff. Jimmy didn't like it, either. Jimmy told Bob to settle down, but he still had to let Bob react to some degree. Because we were winning that first year, we just coped with it as best as we could.

SIGNATURE WIN

We were 2-2 heading into our first Big Eight game. We had to go on the road against 15th-ranked Missouri. At that time, Missouri had a quarterback, Phil Bradley, who later played Major League Baseball, and a running back, James Wilder, who became the Tampa Bay Buccaneers' all-time leading rusher. The Tigers also had a lot of other good players. When they took the field to warm up, you could have put crimson and cream or red and white on them and they would have looked every bit as good as Oklahoma or Nebraska.

We fell behind 13-0 at halftime. It seemed bleak since our starting quarterback and tailback were out with injuries, but we came from behind to win. I think that game propelled Jimmy to become the Big Eight's Coach of the Year that season. It really juiced our fans and let the rest of the league know, "Hey, these guys here, you better watch them!"

John Doerner, a walk-on, played quarterback for us and threw a touchdown pass that was intended for someone else to Ron Ingram. Bob and our offensive coaches caught on to what Missouri was doing defensively and we were able to audible into some plays. It was pretty simple stuff, but we capitalized on it and Terry Suellentrop ran wild for 152 yards.

Defensively, we had our work cut out for us trying to stop Phil Bradley and those backs. But Wannstedt or one of our defensive coaches noticed something that gave away what Missouri planned to do. They were able to move the ball around midfield a lot, but their kicker missed some point-blank field goals and, lo and behold, we won it. That became our signature win.

KANSAS JINX

The Kansas-OSU series was unusual. For 17 years, KU did not beat the Cowboys, although we had a few ties. The two programs were essentially even and, for whatever reason, they just didn't beat us for a long time.

In our first game against the Jayhawks we won 30-17, even though they had receiver David Verser, later a first-round NFL draft pick. Worley Taylor ran for 116 yards and Terry Young, who moved from receiver to running back, got 114 yards on six carries. We made a big goal-line stand and it seems like Billy Wells was one of the guys who helped make the stop.

By this time, we had a 4-3 record even though more than half the players on our two-deep were freshmen or walk-ons.

JIMMY VS. BARRY

How did Jimmy Johnson and Barry Switzer get along when they were Bedlam rivals?

We used to go down to Oklahoma City and socialize with Switzer. One time we went down there and Barry introduced us to the guy involved with those big pyramid schemes. It wasn't illegal, but I didn't know what a pyramid scheme was. There were all these charts and Switzer had us in there showing us that if you did this, you could do this. I was just agreeing. I didn't have any money anyway, but Jimmy had some.

Jimmy and Barry had both played at Arkansas and had been on the staff there. They also coached together at OU. Recruiting became pretty intense at times when we crossed paths, but the coaches at OU and OSU played golf together.

I never had a problem with Barry, although it became fairly interesting later in the pre-probation days. I don't think it's any secret that we both turned each other in on some things. I believe deep down inside we knew we had some kamikaze pilots on both staffs. We never did talk in those terms, but I think we both were a little bit afraid of what was out there. Regardless, we were friends. There was never a confrontation.

FIRST TASTE OF BEDLAM

People claim the Cowboys get more motivated to play the Sooners than vice versa, but let me tell you what I saw in my first Bedlam game.

I remember how gunned up the OU kids were. I remember seeing them come down that ramp. They weren't like, "Hey, this is just another day at the office." They came to play. It wasn't as if they were coming in to play less than their best.

Because of Switzer's personality, I think the perception was that he disrespected Oklahoma State a little bit. People used to tell me, "That doggone Switzer won't acknowledge us." I never did think that. But I know that whatever his kids were told, it got them fired up and they beat us 38-7.

MIRACLE IN THE ROCKIES

The ball bounced our way that first season partially because we made our own breaks. The best example came in a victory over Colorado. They didn't have a very good record, but our coaches worried whether our kids would be mentally ready. They got up on us 20-0 before we could bat an eyelash.

They still led 20-14 with less than four minutes left and, for some reason, they decided to go for it on fourth down at their own 38. If they had punted, we probably weren't going to drive the field and win the game.

Jimmy and I had talked about what we would do in a situation like this and agreed that we would use our goal-line people no matter which end of the field the ball was on.

If they threw the ball, fine. If they got us, they got us. That was the great thing about Jimmy. He never second-guessed us on stuff like that.

Colorado's quarterback, Bill Solomon, tried to sneak for a first down. If I remember correctly, Steve Heinzler and Darryl Sheffey stopped him.

We got the ball, Harold Bailey hit a little play-action pass to Mel Campbell, and we scored with about a minute and a half left to win it.

It was literally the "Miracle in the Rockies." But that's the way that whole season was unfolding for us. At that point, we had three come-from-behind wins.

THE EXAMPLE

Steve Heinzler is still a legend on campus. In fact, the current Oklahoma State head coach, Mike Gundy, brought me over to Stillwater in the spring of 2006 so I could tell his players about Heinzler.

What was so special about Heinzler? He played the majority of the '79 season with casts on his two broken wrists and was still able to make that fourth-down stop against Colorado.

Coming back to play after such injuries, Antle and Heinzler laid the foundation for all those guys that followed. This stuff got passed down from group to group. You want to see what tough is? That's tough.

WINNING SEASON

Worley Taylor ran for 136 yards and three touchdowns to help us beat Kansas State 42-15 in a homecoming game. That allowed us to clinch a winning record while Harold Bailey became OSU's first 1,000-yard passer in eight years.

We finished the season with a 13-10 road victory over Iowa State. Colin Ankerson, who bounced back from a mediocre

---

Harold Bailey, who helped quarterback OSU to a share of the Big Eight title in 1976, revived his career under Jimmy Johnson and Bob Leahy in 1979. *Photo courtesy of Oklahoma State University*

season the year before, hit a 43-yard field goal, his longest of the year, to win the game.

Rick Antle forced a fumble to set up the field goal. He freelanced to make it happen. He was supposed to lock up on the tight end in coverage, but Iowa State ran an option and Rick had enough awareness about him that he left his man and tipped the option pitch. The ball went to the ground and we recovered to win.

In all honesty, we probably would have been content to take a tie for a record of 6-4-1. We still would have felt like world-beaters at the time. Instead we finished 7-4 and third in the Big Eight.

The bus ride from Ames to Des Moines after the game was one of the most satisfying feelings we ever had in our lives. We knew we weren't going to a bowl because of probation, but Jimmy had come in there and juiced the whole thing. We were cheering and singing—the whole deal. You would have thought we were Super Bowl champs. In relative terms, we probably were, and Jimmy was named Big Eight Coach of the Year.

CHAPTER 3

Knocking Their Eyes Out

1980

GREAT EXPECTATIONS

We returned 17 starters from our 7-4 team of 1979, and Jimmy Johnson commented to the press that we were going to knock people's eyes out in 1980.

We probably became a little bit full of ourselves. We were picked to finish third in the Big Eight, which was too high, and we all got wrapped up in the fact that the ball had bounced right the year before.

We had signed a solid recruiting class, including kids like Chris Rockins, Rodney Harding, Kevin Igo, Roderick Fisher, James Spencer, and John Chesley, so enthusiasm was high. But pragmatically, we knew we had some issues with depth on defense and even though our walk-on quarterback, John Doerner, had played in some big wins the year before, we still had some reservations at that position.

TOUGH LESSON

The 1980 opener became one of the biggest coaching fiascos I have ever been involved in. We lost 20-19 at home to West

Texas State, and it taught us a lesson we never forgot in terms of how to prepare for an opener.

We didn't take them lightly, but we outsmarted ourselves offensively and used a lot of audible-type plays. They threw some curveballs at us with their defense and we couldn't handle them. If we had treated the game like a scrimmage and executed our base material, we probably would have pounded out a win. Defensively we battled around, but they exposed a few of our sore spots.

Once the game started, it was a continual bad dream. For a lot of reasons, it became like a nightmare you can't seem to wake up from. It was a hot day. It seemed as if a lot of kids were passing out in the band. The whole thing kicked off very, very badly. West Texas State drove 70 yards on their first drive, then blocked a punt that they converted into a touchdown. It was a complete snowball effect.

Despite it all, we still had a chance to win until Doerner's two-point conversion pass got batted away at the end. But it was just a terrible scene all the way around.

This was a lesson to a lot of us that is still brought up to this day when we talk about season openers.

QUARTERBACK DERBY

After the disappointing season opener, we needed to play somebody we could beat to get back on track. A win would have helped us from a morale standpoint. Instead, we had to play a road game at 17th-ranked Arkansas, which we lost 33-20 even though we snapped the ball twice as many times as they did in the first half.

The score was tied 7-7 at the half and Arkansas scored 19 third-quarter points to change the game.

Doerner fractured a fibula and we had to figure out who would replace him. This was not a great time to lose a quarterback because we were getting ready to play Washington and ranked Missouri and Nebraska teams in succession.

Houston Nutt and Jim Traber were Doerner's backups. They should be familiar names. Nutt is the head football coach at Arkansas. Traber played Major League Baseball for a long time before settling into a career as a sports radio talk show host in Oklahoma City.

Jim has a little bit of pizzazz about him, and I think that's why he's good at what he does today. Back when he was playing, I predicted he would be doing those light beer commercials by the time he was 30. He was a gregarious guy and the defensive coaches liked him because he had some spunk. He was a pretty good talker even back then and had been a very successful multisport high school athlete in Maryland.

Nutt had been a highly recruited high school quarterback in Arkansas and signed with the Razorbacks before transferring to OSU, where he would later become an assistant coach.

Nutt came off the bench against Arkansas when Doerner got hurt and led us to two late touchdowns. The Hog fans booed him because he had transferred out of there.

Traber started the next week with a good day against a good Washington team. He threw for 249 yards and nearly led a comeback to win it, but we fumbled the center exchange near midfield with 1:29 left to lose 24-18. Traber was an excellent hand-eye athlete, but he had small hands, and Nutt began a string of starts the following week.

GETTING OVER THE HUMP

Lopsided losses to Missouri and Nebraska dropped us to 0-5 and we were catching heck for Jimmy's "knock your eyes out" statement.

We tied Kansas in Stillwater, and for some reason, they later forfeited the game. Our first "real" win came in a 15-6 game at San Diego State, the first 100-yard rushing game of Ernest

Anderson's career. The only other notable thing that happened during that road trip was that some of our guys started monkeying around in the surf and had to be rescued. It wasn't anything serious, but they got a little too far away from shore.

DIAMONDS IN THE ROUGH

Even though we beat San Diego State and hammered Colorado 42-7 the next week, the season had become nondescript pretty quick. But it's worth mentioning what Dean Prater accomplished in his time with us.

Prater, who blocked a punt in the Colorado win, had come to OSU as a walk-on and was better than we thought he was. One of the few good things about our loss to Arkansas in 1979 was his emergence in the game. He ended up being a very good player and a classic overachiever. In a season that had gone down the wrong road, he fought his guts out and later played seven years in the NFL.

I wish Dean Prater's story had a happy ending. In 1996, he died after falling in a hotel bathtub. He was one of those Medal of Honor guys.

Also, at some point during the 1980 season, I called Chris Rockins the best freshman defensive player in the Big Eight. And he might have been. We made up our minds going into the season that we were going to bite the bullet and start two raw freshmen, Rockins and Roderick Fisher, at cornerback, because we thought they were going to be outstanding players—and that turned out to be true.

Rockins was eventually a second-round draft pick of the Cleveland Browns. When I signed him out of Sherman, Texas, I almost overlooked him. Sherman had a lot of good, highly recruited players and he was getting lost in the shuffle. Bob Leahy

---

Chris Rockins of Sherman, Texas, was an All-Big Eight cornerback before being selected in the second round of the NFL Draft by the Cleveland Browns. Photo courtesy of Oklahoma State University

pointed out to me that I probably needed to go back to Sherman to look at Rockins again. I did. We beat North Texas to get him and he had an outstanding career. He's still among OSU's all-time leading tacklers.

RECORD DAY

Even though we weren't very good in 1980, we set a defensive record that stood the test of time. In a 10-0 win over Kansas State, we made seven sacks and held them to minus-33 rushing yards, the lowest single-game total ever by an OSU opponent.

REVERSAL OF FORTUNE

Colin Ankerson hit a 43-yard field goal to beat Iowa State in 1979. In the 1980 rematch on a cold, dreary day in Stillwater, Ankerson missed a 42-yarder and we lost 23-21. Jim Traber had come off the bench to lead a touchdown drive and got us in field goal range, but Ankerson missed the kick. A year earlier, he probably would have hit it. But that's kind of the way the whole 1980 season went. It just wasn't happening right.

THE LONGEST WALK

I will never forget our first Bedlam game in Norman for a couple of reasons.

First of all, I remember getting off the bus with the defensive players. This was at a time when players had tickets. Standing right there by the bus is a guy all dressed in red who had some little kids with him. He made some remark asking if we had any tickets. I didn't cuss him or anything, but I just told him we were not in the ticket business.

Instantly, he said to me, "You Aggie-faced blank-blank-blank," and then walked off. He had cussed me like a yard dog.

OU was ranked sixth and they beat us 63-14. We were crippled up and we just wanted to get the game over with quickly.

My future wife, Becky, and Dave Wannstedt's wife, Jan, had driven a car to Norman, and Dave and I planned to ride back to Stillwater with them. The girls met us outside the dressing room. Dave and I still had on our Oklahoma State coaching apparel. So we had to walk with them a pretty good ways over to where the car is parked.

That might have been the longest walk I've ever experienced. It seemed like every time my foot hit the ground, some OU fan was saying something to us. You can imagine what was being said and none of it was any fun. We couldn't hide because we had on our ball gear. I have never been so glad to get in a car. I think Dave and I just lay down in the seat where no one could see us and Becky or Jan drove home.

HINDSIGHT OPINION

We finished the 1980 season with a 4-7 record. Looking back, I don't know if there was anything we could have done about it. We probably had a higher opinion of ourselves than we should have had, but that was kind of Jimmy's nature—and conversely my nature—and I won't say it was wrong.

But we did not think the program was in a bigger hole than we originally envisioned. We were recruiting well and the players we signed after the 1979 and 1980 seasons ended up playing on bowl teams down the road.

A partnership was born after the 1980 season. Jimmy coached in the Blue-Gray game and came away very impressed with a Villanova player named Howie Long. Now they share a Fox Sports studio.

CHAPTER 4

Going Bowling

1981

NUMBERS GAME

Before we delve into the 1981 season, which ended with us going to the Independence Bowl, I've got to tell a recruiting story.

I signed a kid from Dallas named Dirk Davis. He was reasonably highly recruited and I promised him he could have jersey No. 44 if he became a Cowboy.

No big deal, right? Wrong.

At the same time, Dave Wannstedt signed a player from Tulsa Memorial, Doug Maritan, and Wannstedt told the kid he could have jersey No. 44.

How did we get out of that jam? We told both kids they would be listed as No. 44 in preseason and whichever of them played the most early in their first season would get to keep the number.

Dave told me Doug liked 44 so much that he had it on his car. I thought he just had one of those license plates that said "Pokes 44" or something like that. It turned out that Doug had the number on the side of his car, like something you would see in NASCAR. I remember the first time I saw it, I was thinking,

"Oh, Lordy." Dirk ended up with No. 44 because he contributed as a return man right away. I think Doug ended up redshirting. I can't remember whether Doug had the paint job on his car changed or not.

THE ICEMAN COMETH

We opened the 1981 season with a 23-21 win over Tulsa. Jimmy didn't really like playing Tulsa, but there was quite a bit of pressure from our alumni to do so.

Speaking of pressure, it almost never affected our freshman kicker, Larry Roach. He kicked three field goals against Tulsa, including a 24-yard game-winner on the final play.

We fumbled away scoring chances, but John Doerner drove us down into field goal range in the last minute. It was Roach's first college game and he ran out there and kicked it through the uprights. He was an Iceman. I would still take him over anybody if I needed a kick with a game on the line. All he did was set an NCAA freshman record for field goals in '81.

Thank goodness Roach made that kick against Tulsa. We needed to re-establish some positive momentum after coming out of that 1980 season with a bitter taste in our mouths. Even though we lost to San Diego State 23-16 the next week (Shawn Jones, who gained 183 yards, was stopped on a fourth-and-one play at the three in the last minute), we were preparing to launch a pretty good stretch of football.

GUITARS AND FIDDLES

Our third game of the season was against North Texas and we played it in the Cotton Bowl, right in the middle of the Texas State Fair.

North Texas blew it up as a big deal and a country music festival was scheduled after the game. Several "name" people were supposed to play, including Carl Perkins, Kitty Wells, and T.G. Sheppard. Jimmy Johnson joked to reporters following the

matchup that we played like we didn't want people to step on our blue suede shoes.

We won 9-0 and all the points came on Larry Roach field goals. Not very many people saw the game. I remember running out for pregame warmups to see very few people in the Cotton Bowl. The crowd estimate was around 17,000.

GETTING DEFENSIVE

Those who were at the North Texas game saw our defense pitch a shutout. We ended up ninth nationally in total defense that season. That group of guys wasn't as gifted as some of the other teams we had, but they played their guts out. Guy for guy, they might have gotten as much out of themselves as any group we ever had. They were kids like Roderick Fisher, Chris Rockins, Mike Green, Pete DiClementi, Ricky Young, Gary Lewis, and Rodney Harding. They were really starting to come into their own. They made a huge fourth-down stop against North Texas when we guessed right on an option and Gary Lewis, Gary Chachere, and Mike Green dropped their quarterback for a loss. That ended up being a big play to get things started again for us.

The next week, we held Kansas to 15 rushing yards and 125 total yards, beating them 20-7. We stomped them pretty good—and that was a Jayhawk team that made it to a bowl game.

MIRACLE PAYBACK

In our first season at OSU, we pulled off what was called the "Miracle in the Rockies" because we came from behind to beat Colorado up there. They got us back when we returned to Boulder in 1981.

We were up 10-3 with a minute and a half left. We had them backed up at their own eight-yard line with no timeouts. Steve

---

Larry Roach of Dallas was a four-year starting kicker who earned All-Big Eight and All-America honors. *Photo courtesy of Oklahoma State University*

Vogel, who came off the bench when Colorado's starter got hurt in the first half, drove them right down the field and they scored with six seconds left. Colorado went for two and Vogel hit Derek Singleton to win it.

They hadn't done anything all day, but I can remember having a bad feeling once they crossed midfield on that last drive.

Jimmy was mad because he felt like they had run a pick play to get Singleton loose on the two-point conversion. Jimmy tried to plead his case with officials and even drew a diagram of the play for reporters during his postgame talk.

CHANGE IS COMING

We beat Louisville and Missouri in consecutive weeks to improve to 5-2, but our offense was only averaging 16 points a game.

We were glad to get wins however we could get them. But we were moving down a different road offensively and Jimmy wanted to pattern our offense after Nebraska's. That is really not what our offensive coordinator, Bob Leahy, wanted to do, but Jimmy did and he was the boss.

Meanwhile, we got a taste of how good Nebraska's offense could be in '81. They got 54 points on us, and we entered the game ranked about second in total defense.

FEELING RUSTY

We beat Kansas State 31-10 in a homecoming game to clinch a winning season and did it without our starting quarterback and tailback, John Doerner and Shawn Jones, who were out with injuries. Ernest Anderson ran for 139 yards and Rusty Hilger threw for 224 yards in his first collegiate start.

Rusty went on to play for a good while in the NFL, but keep in mind he was the last player in our recruiting class to be offered a scholarship when we signed him.

Rusty had played for Southeast High School in Oklahoma City and Bob Leahy saw something that made him think the kid could be a player.

Hilger started the next game too, throwing two touchdown passes to John Chesley to help us win 27-7 at Iowa State in freezing weather. It was a big win because a bowl bid was at stake. We tried to get a bowl to commit to us before the game. There were only 16 bowls at the time and we wanted to secure an invitation as soon as possible to make sure we weren't left out.

The pregame lobbying failed, but we took care of business on the field. Our defense played like gangbusters. We kept Iowa State to minus-seven rushing yards, sacked their quarterback six times, and held Dwayne Crutchfield, who was the conference's leading rusher, to 26 yards.

HERRING AND BONE

We still had to play OU and both of us had accepted bowl bids, so it wasn't like one team was vastly superior to the other. They beat us 27-3, although the score was a little deceiving.

We played pretty well against their wishbone, holding them to 230 rushing yards. It was the first time we came out of a Bedlam game with something to hang our hats on defensively.

We had done our homework on OU before the season started. A few of us Oklahoma State assistants had gone to Florida State in the spring of '81 to visit with their staff. Florida State had played OU in the two previous Orange Bowls, holding the Sooners to 17 points the last time they met. We borrowed an idea Florida State used against the wishbone, changed it up a little bit, and gave OU some problems the next several years.

The other good thing to come out of that trip was the discovery of Reggie Herring. He had just finished playing at Florida State and was hanging around that spring as a student coach.

Florida State's linebacker coach, Gene McDowell, told us if we were in the market for a graduate assistant, we needed to hire Reggie. Gene let Reggie coach the linebackers that day so we could see Reggie in action. It was like World War III. We went back and told Jimmy we needed to hire this guy. We did and he became a truly outstanding football coach. Now he's the defensive coordinator at Arkansas.

BOWLING IN SHREVEPORT

The 1981 Independence Bowl was OSU's first bowl since 1976 and our first bowl as a staff. We were matched against Texas A&M, which had players like Johnny Hector and Gary Kubiak.

Even though our bowl destination was Shreveport, it was a big deal to us. The Independence Bowl drew the biggest crowd it ever had because it was an easy drive for OSU and A&M fans.

They beat us 33-16 and we finished 7-5. We could have beaten Colorado and San Diego State and won a couple more games, but we were probably about a seven- or eight-win team. We finished third in the Big Eight for the second time in three years, so we felt like we kind of had it going on.

Texas A&M apparently was not as satisfied with the direction of their program. The Aggies fired their coach, Tom Wilson, and hired our old boss, Jackie Sherrill.

CHAPTER 5

Ernest Leads the Nation

1982

GUY TALK

Brent Guy, a former walk-on at OSU, is now the head football coach at Utah State. Brent was a kid who ran for a lot of yards when he played high school ball in Booker, Texas, and just wanted to see if he could play major college football. While at Oklahoma State, he shifted around, from tailback to defensive back and finally to defensive end, where he became a starter in 1982.

Brent had some ability, but was really a classic overachiever. We put him on scholarship and he lettered for three years.

During Brent's time in Stillwater, his girlfriend, who is now his wife, caused a stir. She appeared in a "Girls of the Big Eight" issue of *Playboy*. I want to make it clear that she was clothed. She had shorts and a top on, but she was pictured in that magazine. You can imagine how it was in the locker room. Everybody had the magazine. I was just reading the articles, of course. We all were.

PAT JONES, OFFENSIVE COORDINATOR

Heading into the 1982 season, Jimmy was not pleased with our offense. We had averaged fewer than 300 total yards per game in each of the previous two seasons. Jimmy asked me if I wanted to leave the defense and become offensive coordinator.

There was one problem. We already had an offensive coordinator, Bob Leahy.

Still to this day I am not absolutely sure about it, but I got the impression Jimmy felt Bob would leave of his own free will if I were to become offensive coordinator. Jimmy wouldn't have to fire him.

I think somebody had put a bug in Jimmy's ear that he should put the person he trusted most in charge of the offense. Then Jimmy would call the plays, because, as I mentioned earlier, he wanted to go the direction of Nebraska's offense.

I preferred to stay on defense because we were coming off a pretty good year, but if Jimmy thought a shake-up was the best thing for the team, I was willing to move.

From a staff chemistry standpoint, I had concerns about the title being taken away from Bob and given to me. My fear was, "What if Bob doesn't leave? Then we've got a room full of unhappy campers, or one big-time unhappy camper in that room with me." Jimmy said something to the extent that he would handle it.

Well, Bob didn't leave and we put in the bulk of the Nebraska offense bits and pieces at a time. Jimmy was calling the plays and I was the one structuring it. The biggest beneficiary of the whole deal was Ernest Anderson, who set a school record with 353 rushing attempts and led the country with 1,877 rushing yards in '82.

MOVING ON UP

The staff shake-up helped a couple of our coaches get promotions. Jimmy had asked me if Dave Wannstedt was ready to take over the defense. Dave was a bright guy and I told Jimmy I thought that would be a good move.

Also, we were able to shift graduate assistant Reggie Herring to a full-time position on our defensive staff.

BIG-TIME ADDITIONS

After the 1981 season we signed Leslie O'Neal, who became a three-time All-Big Eight defensive player for us and later had a great career in the NFL.

Leslie was a Little Rock kid who was not interested in going to the University of Arkansas. Leslie went to the same high school I had attended and had an older brother named Leonard who I had coached in high school, but that wasn't why we got him. Butch Davis just did a good job recruiting him. Leslie had a lot of options and I think it came down to UCLA and OSU.

We played Leslie at tight end most of the 1982 season. I don't remember why we put him over there. Jimmy once said the kid could play any position on the field, and he probably could have.

We also got a very good transfer receiver named Jamie Harris from Texas Tech. Jamie had to sit out the '82 season but was worth the wait, leading us in receiving yards each of the next two seasons.

We weren't big on transfers, but this was a kid we knew a lot about since we had recruited him before he signed with Texas Tech. I believe he was the Southwest Conference's freshman of the year or offensive newcomer of the year at Texas Tech, but the next year his father became ill and he had a falling out with the Tech coaches, so he decided to leave.

MUSICAL CHAIRS

Rusty Hilger quarterbacked a few games for us in 1981, but hurt his shoulder before the '82 opener.

Adam Hinds began the season as our starting quarterback, rotating with Ike Jackson. Adam was a transfer from Principia

College who was athletic enough to be offered a basketball scholarship by the University of New Orleans when he was in high school.

Adam eventually lost the starting job to Ike, whose arm was so strong that he could throw a ball through a building. Adam was a classy kid and we moved him to defense the next season. We had to find a place for him to play, so he took over free safety for us and did it well, ranking among the nation's interception leaders. But with the quarterback situation a kind of a musical chairs deal in '82, we had all the more reason to hand the ball to Ernest Anderson.

ERNEST GETS ROLLING

Our spirits were pretty high because we had 17 starters back from our Independence Bowl team. We won the '82 season opener 27-6 over North Texas State even though we gave the ball away seven times.

Ernest Anderson scored on a 74-yard run our first play. That was more than North Texas gained against us all day. The Mean Green managed 71 total yards.

Ernest ran for 220 yards, setting the tone for what he would do that season. We were running the devil out of the power play. Tony Wise did a good job with the offensive linemen. Those guys knew what they were doing and Ernest's instincts were good.

Ernest was a workhorse and we were not scared we would wear him out because he had played fullback before, plus he was stout. We just kept pounding him in there.

Ernest gained 152 yards against Tulsa the next week. If we could have gotten him a couple more yards, we might have won. We had a first and goal at the three with Tulsa leading 19-15. We

---

Adam Hinds was a transfer from Principia College who first played quarterback, then became a leader in a very talented secondary. He was drafted by the Miami Dolphins.
Photo courtesy of Oklahoma State University

didn't get it in the end zone, although Jimmy thought Ernest got in on one of those goal-line plays.

The game was a crusade for Tulsa as they nabbed four interceptions and beat us 25-15. We all had a rotten feeling on that bus ride back home.

Ernest ran for 195 yards in our third game and moved past Eric Dickerson to become the national rushing leader, but Louisville drove 86 yards in three plays for a clinching touchdown to beat us 28-22.

Louisville had a pretty good receiver. Mark Clayton, who caught four balls for 152 yards against us that road game, later became a five-time Pro Bowler with the Miami Dolphins.

FIT TO BE TIED

Despite Ernest's success, we had trouble winning enough games to get over the hump. In fact, we produced an oddity by playing in back-to-back tie games.

Ernest ran for 270 yards, a school record at the time, in a 24-24 tie with Kansas. We were up 24-10, but a fake punt blew up on us and the Jayhawks capitalized on the momentum shift. Ike Jackson became the first quarterback to go the distance for us in a game that season.

The next week, Ernest ran for 205 yards and we outgained Colorado 487-215, yet we had to settle for a 25-25 tie. Ike threw five picks but led us back from a 22-10 deficit to put us up by three in the fourth quarter. In the last 32 seconds, Colorado quarterback Randy Essington passed the Buffaloes into position for a tying field goal.

We had the nation's leading rusher and we thought we were a good football team, but our record was 1-2-2.

MOUNT RUSH-MORE

Ernest Anderson reached a milestone in 1982 when he became the fourth player in major college history to rush for 1,000 yards in the first five games of a season.

Bedlam was next. There was quite a bit of Ernest vs. Marcus Dupree build-up. It became one of only two games that season in which Ernest was held below 100 yards, but we still hung in there against an OU team ranked 20th.

We were behind only 13-9 when we fumbled a punt that they recovered at our 12 to set up a Dupree touchdown run late in the third quarter. OU got another touchdown in the fourth quarter and won 27-9. The Bedlam game the previous year helped to turn things around, making our kids believe they were good enough to win, and this was essentially an even game for a long time.

Ernest gained 227 yards the next week in a 30-20 win over Missouri, but cracked a rib in the fourth quarter and was only able to get 68 yards in a 48-10 loss to sixth-ranked Nebraska.

PLAYING SPOILER

Even though the '82 season didn't go the way we wanted, we got things together toward the end of the season and beat the first bowl team in Kansas State history.

Jim Dickey redshirted his senior class in '81 in order to have a shot at success in '82. It was one of the more gutsy moves that I saw in our league—just to massively redshirt a group of guys—and I thought it was a mistake when Kansas State let Jim go a couple of years later.

Kansas State had already clinched its first winning season since 1970 by the time we played them. They would go on to lose to Wisconsin in the Independence Bowl.

Anderson ran for 175 yards against the Wildcats and we scored 17 fourth-quarter points in a 24-16 victory. Rod Brown clinched it with an interception in the last minute.

HOT AND COLD

We finished with our best game of the season—a 49-13 win over Iowa State—and our worst game of the season—a 35-6 loss to San Diego State—in consecutive weeks.

San Diego State threw for a jillion yards on us. I remember we just wanted to get the game over with and get out of there. Ernest and Ken Zachary both ran for more than 100 yards against Iowa State and Ernest ran for 146 against San Diego State to ease past Georgia's Heisman Trophy winner, Herschel Walker, for the national rushing title.

The win over Iowa State helped us get to 3-2-2 in league play and we finished third in the Big Eight for the third time in four seasons. So even though this turned out to be a disappointing year, some good things happened. One was positive national publicity. *Sports Illustrated* did a feature on Ernest. It wasn't a cover story, but it was the first major article in *Sports Illustrated* since our staff had been there.

Our overall record was 4-5-2. We knew we were a better football team than that, but we did things that wouldn't allow us to win, like averaging 3.1 turnovers a game.

GOODBYE, OFFENSE

After that season, I told Jimmy Johnson that I regretted my only season as offensive coordinator. It was not a fun year for me. If I had it to do all over again, I wouldn't do it. With Bob Leahy still there, the tension continued. Resentment was brewing. It was just not good. There were no big blow-ups, but Jimmy knew that it was hard, that I didn't like it, and that I didn't feel comfortable. I don't think the other coaches were comfortable

---

Ernest Anderson, who played tailback and fullback during his career, was an All-American in 1982, when he led the nation in rushing.
Photo courtesy of Oklahoma State University

with it either, but we just bored through it. I was happy to move back to defense the next season.

CHAPTER 6

Battling the Big Red Machine

1983

SHAKING THINGS UP

Jimmy Johnson had a brief flirtation with Tulane after the 1982 season. His contract extension was announced afterward. But Jimmy was getting pressure from the regent level to make some staff changes—or at least that's what we thought.

I wanted to go back to defense, but I didn't want the title of defensive coordinator to be taken away from Dave Wannstedt. I was very sensitive to his feelings because I liked him and I didn't want to undercut him. If it had been somebody I didn't feel quite so strongly about, I don't think it would have bothered me. But I probably would have left rather than cost Dave his title. I went so far as to talk with the Kansas City Chiefs about a linebacker job. The Chiefs ended up offering it to someone else, but I was in the mix.

Jimmy apparently had some kind of staff-juggling plan that we weren't privy to. But everything worked out. Dave, knowing that things were getting tight in Stillwater, went to USC and reunited with Frank Faulks, who had once been on our staff.

After Dave became the second OSU assistant coach to go to USC, Jimmy got mad. Ted Tollner was cherry-picking our staff.

Jimmy told Ted something that can't be sugarcoated enough to print in this book.

Then other dominoes start falling. Larry Holton, who had been moved from defense to offense, left to take a job at Tennessee and stayed there maybe a day before he went to Illinois.

Jimmy had already told Bob Leahy he would have to go. Leahy later wound up on the USFL staff of former OSU coach Jim Stanley.

HELP WANTED

Jimmy had to hire four coaches to complete our staff. The new guys were George Walstad, Larry Coker, Bill Shimek, and Willie Anderson.

We hired Coker away from the University of Tulsa to run the offense. Jimmy and Tulsa's coach, John Cooper, sparred a little, but we always had a great deal of respect for what Larry and their coaches had done offensively with their program. We liked Larry. He was a veteran guy and highly regarded in the Oklahoma high school ranks. Jimmy didn't give him the title of coordinator that first year, but Larry was the coordinator whether he had the title or not. Of course, Larry would later win a national championship as head coach at Miami, Florida.

Walstad, a former OSU player, was at Wyoming when we hired him. Kansas State's Jimmy Dickey gave George a good recommendation. George once coached under Dickey, who said George was the only coach he ever really hated to lose. George was a veteran guy who knew how to coach and recruit and, on top of that, he had OSU ties. So we hired him. George was instrumental a few years later in our finding a recruit named—maybe you've heard of him—Barry Sanders.

Shimek was a former Arkansas high school coach who went to OU when one of his players signed with them. Jimmy Johnson knew Shimek, who had signed great Sooner running backs like Billy Sims and David Overstreet.

Somehow there had been some reshuffling at OU, and Shimek went from being the running backs coach to helping somebody with the running backs. I talked to Bill about joining us and he was interested. Jimmy was getting tired of hiring coaches. That can wear a guy down. Finally, one afternoon, Jimmy asked if I still felt good about Shimek. I told him I thought he could help us. I found Shimek down at Oak Tree playing golf and we hired him.

CURLEY OR WILLIE?

We were still one coach short of a full staff heading into spring practice and we wanted to hire a minority coach. I remember we brought in Curley Culp, who had played at Arizona State and had been a Pro Bowler in the NFL.

Somebody had recommended Culp to Jimmy. We brought Culp in and he was a nice guy, but had never coached and had zero recruiting experience. Jimmy was really torn because we liked him. But we wanted somebody that could recruit and had a little experience, especially since recruiting was pretty vicious during this era.

Jimmy kept on getting calls about the staff vacancy and a lot of people told Jimmy he should consider hiring Clemson's Willie Anderson. Willie had some NCAA problems before, but somebody Jimmy trusted was among those who lobbied on Willie's behalf.

This was all happening at the same time I was traveling to Georgia with our secondary coach, Paul Jette. We went there to pick the brain of Bill Lewis, one of the best secondary coaches I have ever been around. He was a great zone defense coach and that was the same stuff we were really going to sink our teeth into.

Anyhow, Jimmy told Jette and me that he wanted us to meet Willie Anderson near the Atlanta airport while we were out in Georgia. It was a semi-job interview. Jimmy just wanted us to get a feel for Willie. We sat down with him at a restaurant near the airport and talked for a pretty long while.

Later, Jimmy asked us for an opinion on Willie. We gave a middle of the road answer. We didn't really want to torpedo the guy. But it wasn't a matter of us coming back as we did with Reggie Herring, saying, "Here's the guy we've got to hire." It wasn't that. But we didn't want to go back and say this guy was no good, either.

I don't remember us bringing Willie in for an official interview. I think we just hired him. It was more like, "You've got the job, get on over here, and let's start spring drills."

THE MIAMI DEFENSE

People talk about the Miami defense, a built-for-speed approach that the Hurricanes used to win national championships. That style of defense was born in Stillwater in 1983.

Our coaches had to scramble to put something together when Jim Krebs, our junior college All-America linebacker signee, broke an arm in two-a-days. Krebs was a legit middle linebacker in our 4-3 defense and you've got to really know what you are doing to play that position.

I remember talking with Jimmy after Krebs got hurt. We said, "We've got to change our scheme without changing too much." We lined a guy up over the center and shaded him, but kept elements of our 4-3. We moved Matt Monger to an inside linebacker position and it was natural for him, because the center was covered and Matt could just run.

Some of this was old stuff that Jimmy and his crew had done with the Monster defense at Arkansas. But we could still keep our coverages intact and we changed the technique of one of our ends, which proved to be a big key in regard to a significant personnel move. In fact, let's interrupt this story so I can tell you about Warren Thompson.

PACKAGE DEAL

Warren Thompson made a million plays for us in this new defense. His emergence proved that recruiting is an inexact science.

Here's what I mean: we recruited a junior college running back named Joe Miller, who once had been a Washington D.C.-area high school player of the year. To get Joe, we also signed his buddy, Warren Thompson. It was a calf-cow deal.

Joe Miller never played much, but that was because we always had a lot of other good players at his position.

Warren looked like he could be a safety or a linebacker—just a tall, rangy kid that could run. Once we changed that technique for one of our ends, it gave an inexperienced, raw guy like Warren a chance to play the position and make a difference. All he did was fire his gun down inside. There wasn't much technique, just go. Once we made that change, Warren started showing up all over creation in practices.

MAKING PIECES FIT

We had John Washington and Leslie O'Neal populating our defensive line, but we were still about one lineman short and the season opener was just around the corner.

The question, "Can we get Warren Thompson on the field?" was raised during a staff meeting. We decided to move Rodney Harding inside with O'Neal and Washington. That allowed Thompson, who had been listed as Harding's backup, to get in the lineup.

I think that personnel move set the tone of this defense for about the next two years. We kept it very simple for Warren and he became a playmaker. Rodney Harding was a proven

John Washington, All-American Leslie O'Neal, and Rodney Harding formed one of the greatest pass rush trios in Big Eight history.
Photo courtesy of Oklahoma State University

playmaker. It totally got us our best people out there on the field. Everything you hear people talk about today concerning speed and quickness and this particular style of defense that has been coined the Miami defense—this group started it.

It wasn't revolutionary, but it was combining together some things that were a little bit different. Just changing a couple of shades, moving a guy out, and moving a guy in gave people all kinds of trouble. Plus, we had a bunch of rockets like James Ham out there. We had some guys that could really go and we played well enough in '83 to rank eighth nationally in rushing defense and ninth in scoring defense.

Obviously, when Jimmy left to go to Miami, he took this defense with him.

If Jim Krebs doesn't break his arm in two-a-days, does any of this happen? Probably not.

TEST DRIVE

We were still feeling our way around with this defense in our season opener against North Texas State. I don't think they ever really moved the ball on us, and we won 20-13. Harding forced a fumble that O'Neal recovered, setting up a 46-yard Shawn Jones touchdown run with a little over five minutes to go.

GRAND THEATER

Paul Jette and I visited with Georgia's staff the previous spring about secondary coverages, but we also picked up some other information that proved to be helpful. We had not played many night games, but Georgia's coach, Vince Dooley, apparently liked to settle his team down for night kickoffs by taking them to movies on the day of the game. We were hunting for a routine, so we took their advice.

I don't want to give a movie credit for a win, but we saw a motion picture the day we had to play a night road game against a Cincinnati team that had just beaten Penn State. I think seeing that movie—I believe it was a kung fu flick—made us more comfortable.

We scored all our points in the second half and came from behind for a 27-17 win. Ernest Anderson didn't play because of a groin injury, but Shawn Jones rushed for 160 yards and our fullback, Kelly Cook, ran for 96.

The game was supposed to be at Riverfront Stadium and we hoped it would be, because playing at a pro arena might convince our kids to take the game more seriously. The game got moved to a campus stadium because the Cincinnati Reds staged Pete Rose Night at Riverfront. Cincinnati's stadium was slam full that night, but we played a dime package and intercepted three passes to spoil it for their fans.

FAMILIAR FACE

Three members of our Oklahoma State staff—Jimmy, Tony Wise, and I—had to face our old boss, Jackie Sherrill, in the third game of the 1983 season. We were all working together at Pitt before Jackie left to become the head coach at Texas A&M.

Tony Wise and I roomed together on the road and were just killing time before that game against A&M. I remember Tony asking me what I thought would happen and I said, "Tony, if we play good, I think we are going to beat their brains out." That took Tony by surprise, but I felt comfortable saying it because we were becoming tough defensively.

Shawn Jones ran for 203 yards and Rusty Hilger threw two touchdown passes to Jamie Harris. We won 34-15 and it was a big win in a lot of ways, especially since we recruited so much in Texas.

Defensively, we continued to play lights out and pitched a 9-0 shutout at Tulsa the following week. We were 4-0 for the first time since 1975. Our next two games were against top-ranked Nebraska and 15th-ranked Oklahoma.

BIG RED DYNASTY

Sports Illustrated called Nebraska "the best team in college football history" in 1983. I still think it's the greatest offensive team I've ever seen. Just look at who was on that offense: Turner Gill was a great college quarterback; Mike Rozier won the Heisman; Irving Fryar was a first-round pick; and Dean Steinkuhler won the Lombardi Award and the Outland Trophy. They were beating people by an average score of 58-11 before we played them.

Jamie Harris of McKinney, Texas, transferred from Texas Tech and was a legitimate big-play threat who led the Cowboys in receiving in 1983 and 1984. *Photo courtesy of Oklahoma State University*

The "Big Red Machine" was on the cover of *Sports Illustrated* the week the Huskers came to Stillwater. It may have been the most exciting game we ever had in the 16 years I was at Oklahoma State. We were all just quivering when it was over, because we had had a legitimate chance to beat a team that would go undefeated in the regular season and play Miami for the national championship in the Orange Bowl.

We led 10-7 at the half—I'm sure that score sent shock waves around the country—and lost 14-10. We were throwing passes in the end zone at the end with a chance to pull off the greatest upset in school history.

Say what you want about moral victories, but this one was. We were trying to say the right things and that there are no moral victories, but we knew it was. This game set the tone for the season. We were 4-0 before the game and people were wondering, "Who are these guys? Are they any good?" Well, yeah, we were good.

TIGER BLITZ

Jimmy told us to do anything we could to slow down Nebraska. We didn't think we could hold up against them because we were not big enough.

Initially, we were going to copy the defense North Texas used against us in the opener. They played almost a nine-man front that bothered us. We were going to throw caution to the wind and try it, but we didn't really know what we were doing and it looked awful during a Monday practice.

I told that to Jimmy and he said, "Do whatever you want." Instead of copying North Texas, we borrowed from Missouri.

Nebraska beat Missouri 6-0 in 1981 and Missouri limited the Huskers to six points just lining up and blitzing the devil out of them. We put that same blitz in, fit it to us, and called it Tiger Blitz. Then we put in another blitz in which we would ultimately fire the cornerback.

We were going to call one of the two blitzes every down. We were going to fake one of them and do the other. That's all we practiced. And we were not a big blitz team.

The game arrived. We lined up for the first play on defense and called Tiger Blitz. They tossed it to Rozier and two defenders hit him for a four- or five-yard loss.

Next we called corner fire and Rockins sacked Turner Gill. We hadn't worked much on long-yardage situations because we didn't think it would be that kind of game. But we went to our dime defense, we blitzed Mike Hudson from one side and Mark Moore from the other, and they got to Turner Gill.

The Big Red Machine had been hit in the teeth. Everyone in the place stood up. I don't know that anybody sat down the rest of the day.

Gill threw a 62-yard pass to Fryar for a touchdown and Nebraska got a 42-yard reverse during a 92-yard touchdown drive, but they could not run their base offense against us.

We used the Tiger Blitz and corner fire against them every year for a long time. We went two consecutive years without allowing them a rushing touchdown against us. We made them hit the throws. They finally hit a few and ran a punt back on us one year, but as far as gnawing us up on the run, huh-uh. We had 'em.

OU held Nebraska to 28 points that year, but other than that game and the one against us, the rest of the Cornhuskers' regular-season games were not even close. It was the most exciting game I think I ever saw in Stillwater, and it was probably the best defensive effort against quality people that I was ever associated with in any shape, form, or fashion.

It was also a coming-out party for Leslie O'Neal. I think Nebraska had a starter down in the offensive line and O'Neal completely ate up the replacement. He got a sack right before the half on a down when we didn't blitz. People were starting to understand that O'Neal, a true sophomore, was something special, and people were beginning to realize we had a very, very good football team.

BEDLAM HEARTBREAK

After nearly upsetting Nebraska in an emotional game, how would we bounce back the next week against Oklahoma? We got the answer when we built a 20-3 lead.

We led by that score early in the fourth quarter and some of our assistants raised the question as to when we should start letting subs play.

I said, "Whoa, don't do that. Leave our starters out there, let's beat these people, and we will talk about it tomorrow." I honestly felt that, the way our defense was playing, we could play that Sooner team for a year and they wouldn't have scored on us. They converted two of 15 third downs against us.

Then something bad happened. Two of our starting defensive backs ran together and what would have been about a 10-yard pass for OU went 73 yards for a touchdown.

If we could have made a first down at any time, the game probably would have been over, but they scored 18 points in the last 10 minutes and beat us 21-20.

OU recovered a bizarre onside kick to set up a game-winning field goal. There was a mix-up in their communication, so everybody on OU's team thought Tim Lashar was going to kick the ball deep. Instead, Lashar booted a line drive onside kick that hit Chris Rockins in the helmet and they recovered.

If Rockins had moved his head six inches, the game would have been over. Rockins was a great player for us and later a second-round NFL draft pick. People remember his role in this onside kick, but they probably forget he recovered an onside kick to help us clinch a season-opening win over North Texas. We had our "hands" team out there for the onside kick against OU, but fate just totally took hold of that one.

LIFESAVER

We were disappointed that we lost the Bedlam game, but the outcome may have saved a life.

Gary Gibbs, OU's defensive coordinator at the time and later head coach, told me later on he was one step away from jumping out of the press box when we built that big lead.

If we had beaten them, their boosters were going to raise hell and they might start to run off all the coaches. They were in a bit of a recession at the time and the Marcus Dupree mess had begun. Gary told me, "I just wanted to jump out of the press box and hit the pavement down there."

PLAYING HURT

Ernest Anderson, who led the nation in rushing in 1982, didn't have the same kind of year in 1983 because he was hurt quite often. He missed four games following the opener and was then hospitalized with a bleeding ulcer after carrying the ball 11 times against OU.

Even though Ernest didn't get out of the hospital until Wednesday of game week, he ran for 131 yards in our 27-10 win over Kansas a few days later. It's no wonder a recruit named Thurman Thomas admired the guy.

BLITZKRIEG

Colorado came from behind to beat us in 1981 and rallied to tie us in 1982, but we blitzed the dog out of them and beat them 40-14 in '83.

We knew from watching film that we could blitz them into submission if they didn't do anything differently. Basically we just rolodexed four blitzes. We were on them so quick that the ball was getting batted around, and their quarterback, Steve Vogel, missed his first seven throws and got benched. We scored 30 second-quarter points and had them blown away by halftime.

Jimmy let us do what we wanted as far as those blitzes. Was he always so willing to be hands off? If he thought we knew what we were doing, he was. And that was the beauty of my coaching defense with Jimmy, because we were always on the same page. I can't remember a disagreement.

R-E-S-P-E-C-T

We had a 6-2 record and could have been 8-0 if we had capitalized on opportunities to beat OU and Nebraska. It came up during our weekly press conference that maybe we should be ranked. Then we lost 21-20 at home to Kansas State and 16-10 on the road against Missouri.

Kansas State just did better schematically against our defense than anybody else did that season and got two long drives against us. There was a little bit of a controversy on K-State's winning drive. Rodney Harding caused a fumble, but an official said the ball was dead. We still had a chance to win, but Larry Roach was short on a 58-yard field goal attempt at the end.

Harry Roberts returned the opening kickoff 90 yards for a touchdown against Missouri, but we could not move the ball on them a lick and gave up a 10-0 lead.

CLOSE CALLS

At this point we were 6-4 and our four losses were by a combined 12 points. Without stretching it at all, we could have been 10-0.

Jimmy was so disheartened after the Missouri game that he went home after his TV show. But good news was a phone call away.

One of our graduate assistants popped in while some of our coaches were meeting and said, "The athletic director, Myron Roderick, needs to speak with you."

Myron asked if Jimmy was around and then asked me if we wanted to go to the Bluebonnet Bowl in Houston. The

Bluebonnet Bowl didn't even want to wait until we had played Iowa State in the last game of the regular season. They were ready to take us right away.

I told Myron to inform the Bluebonnet Bowl we were coming and I would go tell Jimmy. I told Jimmy and he asked, "Are you kidding me?" because, like me, he thought we might have to beat Iowa State just to go somewhere like the Independence Bowl. The Bluebonnet Bowl was a good bowl, but somebody had bailed out on them. They were in a pickle and needed a team that was going to bring some fans. We accepted the invitation and we were ecstatic about it.

MARKED MAN

Mark Moore was not a highly recruited guy, but Reggie Herring was high on him and we signed him. Mark became a two-time All-America defensive back and was, pound for pound, maybe the most violent hitter we had at Oklahoma State. If you were going to pick somebody to spend the night with in a foxhole, Mark would be at the top of that list.

Mark was not a violent guy—in fact, he was extremely polite and he was one of the leaders of that good-guy group—but he was incredibly tough and he would just completely kill you when he hit you. He once hit a kid from Nebraska so hard that it knocked the guy back under a TV truck and literally silenced Memorial Stadium in Lincoln.

In our game against Iowa State in 1983, Paul Jette came up with the idea of playing a box-and-one defense against Iowa State. Mark shadowed their best receiver, Tracy Henderson, for virtually the entire game. Henderson caught a school-record 16 passes the week before against Kansas State, but Mark just ate Henderson's lunch, holding him to two catches for 16 yards.

We played two-deep around the box-and-one and rushed three players. We played it every down with the exception of short yardage and, to this day, Iowa State still hasn't figured it out.

Their quarterback, David Archer, set records that season, but he only got 116 passing yards against us.

Some of the assistant coaches were at a watering hole toasting ourselves after we got back to Stillwater. Jimmy called us and said, "I thought I could coach defense, but you guys can really coach defense."

JIMMY LEAVING?

Jimmy flirted with a couple of jobs late in the '83 season. I think Jimmy had gotten a little cross with a couple of regents on some issue and there had been another problem. Before Myron Roderick was hired as athletic director, Jimmy and our faculty representative had said they might want to handle A.D. chores if the university couldn't find exactly the right person. Jimmy liked Myron, but I don't know if Jimmy took it seriously that Myron might become the athletic director. And then that all went down.

Jimmy wanted to leave. He wanted to go. Why? That's his business. But I think being in a small town was getting to him a little. He knew this might be the time to jump. He had an opportunity to strike. He had formed a pretty good football team and now had a chance to go.

Rice had a vacancy and Jimmy checked that out. I was trying to talk him out of it. We had just rebuilt the OSU program. "Do we really want to go down there and try to rebuild Rice? Why do you want to rebuild again where you are staring Texas in the face? We've got to stare OU in the face at Oklahoma State, but at least we've got better players than Rice."

Rice was in the Southwest Conference, which appealed to Jimmy. Ultimately, Rice hired Watson Brown, the brother of current Texas coach Mack Brown. I can't speak for Jimmy, but I

Mark Moore of Nacogdoches, Texas, was a two-time All-American from 1985 to 1986 and one of the fiercest hitters in Big Eight history.
Photo courtesy of Oklahoma State University

do think he would have gone to Rice if they had come to him and said, "You're our guy." That's my gut feeling.

The other possibility was Arkansas. After our game against Iowa State, somebody called me at home and told me Lou Holtz had resigned at Arkansas, Jimmy's alma mater.

Arkansas flew over here, picked up Jimmy and Linda Kay, and took them to Fayetteville in the school plane, where Jimmy and Frank Broyles, Arkansas' longtime athletic director, got kind of cross. We later found out Ken Hatfield had already been there and had been told the job was his, or something of that nature. They probably brought Jimmy over there just to pacify Jerry Jones. Jimmy was incredibly upset at Coach Broyles because he thought he had been used.

SETTING THE STAGE

At about the same time all of this was happening, Jimmy gave me the title of assistant head coach.

To this day, I think Jimmy knew he was going to leave. He didn't know where, but he was going somewhere. By giving me the title, he had set it up for me to be the next head coach. He did the same thing later for Dave Wannstedt when we were all with the Miami Dolphins.

JIMMY'S FAREWELL

Jimmy's last game as head coach was a 24-14 win over No. 20 Baylor in the Bluebonnet Bowl.

It was a great experience. I remember the team going to a pregame movie at the Galleria in Houston. The place was slam full of Oklahoma State people. It was like the parting of the Red Sea when the squad came through.

We had great practices down there. A lot of people didn't do conditioning for bowl games, but we ran all the time. Once at the Astrodome, we are doing one of our conditioning drills when we got to cooking with this group. It was pretty impressive. We were whooping and hollering and cutting loose when Baylor entered the top of the stadium. They looked at us and we had stallions. I remember Baylor standing up there almost marveling at us. They didn't know what they were fixing to get into with our group.

We went out on the field and got after Baylor pretty good. Rusty Hilger threw two touchdown passes, but only played one half because he got knocked out of the game. Ernest Anderson ran for 134 yards and, even though Baylor was pretty good offensively (one of their rotating quarterbacks was Cody Carlson), we still took care of them.

RODNEY'S RAP

Rodney Harding was a real football player. He didn't say a lot and he wasn't a loud guy, but when he talked, people listened.

The night before the Bluebonnet Bowl, we held our defensive meeting with coaches and players. At certain points, we went around the room, asking guys if they wanted to say anything. Rodney stood up and said something to the effect of, "If I live for however many more years, I will never forget this group, ever. I can't explain how much you guys mean to me."

We were standing there, all of us in that room, and we all had something in our eyes. It was one of those deals. Everybody in that room knew we were going to beat Baylor. But the whole week was kind of magic in that regard. Everything just went exactly as it needed to go, except when Ike Jackson threw an interception late in the game. Coaches suspected he threw it on purpose and Jimmy was mad as hell at him. We knew Ike was going to leave, which he did after that ballgame. So did Jimmy, a few months later.

CHAPTER 7

Goodbye Jimmy, Hello Mr. Iba

CHAIN REACTION

Howard Schnellenberger coached Miami, Florida, to a national championship in 1983. The Hurricanes beat Nebraska in the Orange Bowl when the Huskers, instead of kicking a tying extra point, failed on a two-point conversion attempt.

Schnellenberger resigned after the end of the '83 season to become head coach of the USFL's Washington Federals, who were supposed to relocate to South Florida. The deal fell through and Schnellenberger never coached a down in the USFL.

The ripples of Schnellenberger's exit were felt all the way to Stillwater.

Jimmy Johnson and Tulsa's John Cooper got involved in the hunt for Schnellenberger's old job at Miami.

Jimmy didn't say much about what was going on with the Miami situation, but I remember we were at a cocktail function in Western Oklahoma when Jimmy told an OSU booster, "Whatever happens, I want you to take care of him." And Jimmy pointed to me. I didn't know exactly what that meant, but I had a suspicion.

As the Miami matter became more public, Jimmy called all of the assistant coaches into a staff meeting and said he didn't know what would happen. He also told us everybody was going to be taken care of. Nothing was said beyond that.

LAYING THE GROUNDWORK

I told Jimmy that I wasn't asking his business in regard to the Miami job, but if something was getting ready to happen, he should let me know so I could begin trying to get the head coaching job at Oklahoma State. I think at that point he told me to go ahead and start. I knew then that wheels were in motion.

Jimmy called me later and told me to come over to his house. Charlie Drake, the attorney and legal counsel for OSU, was there with his wife and they were having drinks. I could tell that something was coming down since they were in a festive mood.

The phone rang and it was Sam Jankovich, Miami's athletic director. I could tell that Sam was saying something like, "I am going to put Tad Foote, the university president, on the phone and he is going to offer you this job." It was a done deal at that point. Jimmy was excited and told them he would be there the next day for a press conference. I left because I didn't feel comfortable just sitting around having a party. I was fixing to go do my thing so I could get a head start pursuing the OSU job.

ADVICE FROM A LEGEND

As soon as I left Jimmy Johnson's house, I didn't call an agent or an attorney. I didn't see the president or the athletic director. I went directly to Mr. Iba's house.

Mr. Iba is Henry Iba, a legendary former Oklahoma State and U.S. Olympic basketball coach. Everybody called him Mr. Iba because he commanded that kind of respect.

Did Mr. Iba have more clout than everybody else? I didn't really know that, but I trusted him. Maybe I didn't know any better. But we had a good relationship. He liked me. I knew that.

I felt comfortable enough with him that I went directly from Jimmy's house and knocked on Mr. Iba's door. I thought that, of every living being on the planet, Mr. Iba was Oklahoma State. And I was right.

I told Mr. Iba what was happening and asked him how I could get the OSU job.

He told me to sit down and gave me two pieces of advice: don't try to get the job through the media; and let your friends get the job for you.

I said, "Fair enough. What do you want me to do? Should I go see the athletic director?" Mr. Iba told me not to do anything until he told me otherwise. I went home and called our friend Kevin Leonard, the oilman in Oklahoma City who helped Jimmy get the OSU job. But I didn't want to call too many people. I was a little afraid of the media and I was totally in agreement with Mr. Iba that you don't get jobs through them.

DIVIDE AND CONQUER

After I told Mr. Iba what was going on, he got on the phone and called two or three of his buddies. They were all his vintage of guys, older guys. Mr. Iba grabbed a game program and opened it to the page with the board of regents. One would point to different regents, saying, "I will take him, him, and her." And somebody else would say, "I can get to him, him, and her." They divided them up to campaign on my behalf.

I already had the title of assistant head coach and, when news broke that Jimmy was leaving, I called the other coaches together. I don't remember having a staff meeting as such, but guys were coming around. None of the other coaches had seniority. I was the only one on the staff who was going to get the job. The other coaches came up with a plan to help. I think some of them might have gone to the players and had them start a petition for me.

It must have been the next day when Mr. Iba came over. He saw me and said he was going to go visit with Myron Roderick, the athletic director. I don't know exactly what was said, but I saw Myron later and let it be known that I wanted the job. You get concerned in these kinds of situations because somebody usually wants to open up the search. Myron just told me not to do anything and that was about all that was said.

MAKING IT OFFICIAL

It wasn't very long before the regents called a special meeting in Oklahoma City. Myron went down there to recommend that they hire me. He wanted me present too, just in case they wanted to talk to me.

Ed Ketchum was the chairman of the board of regents. He was a good guy, but a little bit volatile at times. Myron told me that Ed wanted to meet me, so I met Ed and his wife at a restaurant at the Holiday Inn out by Frontier City, the amusement park in Oklahoma City. We only talked for about five minutes. I just think Ed wanted to be able to go into that board of regents meeting saying he had met me.

I went from there to Kevin Leonard's house. Sometime that night Myron called and asked, "Do you want to be the head coach?"

I said, "Yes, sir." I called George Walstad and told him I had become the head coach and asked him to call everybody else.

STAFF TUNE-UP

As Myron and I drove back from Oklahoma City, I bounced some thoughts off him. Larry Coker technically did not have the title of offensive coordinator, even though he was, so I wanted to make it official. I also wanted to make Paul Jette the defensive coordinator to take my place and George Walstad the assistant head coach.

The only one of our coaches who had left town was Butch Davis. He was over in Arkansas playing in a golf tournament, an annual deal, with one of his buddies from Springdale. I told

Myron I would like to think about giving Willie Anderson the title of recruiting coordinator. Butch held the title. I had nothing against Butch, but was enamored with Willie's work habits, the chance to promote a minority guy, and the opportunity to give him a title.

Butch was afraid of the title change. I told him not to read anything into it. I just wanted to do it for Willie. I probably hurt Butch's feelings, but I wasn't trying to do that.

HELP WANTED

Jimmy told Myron he wouldn't try to hire anybody from the OSU staff. The other side of it was that Jimmy had been told to retain his Miami staff, and he knew that before he took the job. Some real horror stories came out of that. Three of the Miami assistants had tried to get the head coaching job, so it was not a good scene for Jimmy. There were bad vibes and staff chemistry was not ideal.

A couple of our assistants, Paul Jette and Reggie Herring, went down there to visit Miami. When they came back, Paul told me he was going to stay. Reggie had actually cleaned out his office, then he walked down to his car and changed his mind. He put all his stuff back in the office. Reggie is a pretty impulsive guy.

Jimmy was having a hard time hiring a defensive line coach, and Butch Davis, who was going to coach receivers for us, wanted to coach defense. So Butch agreed to go down there with Jimmy, which turned out to be a good move for Butch since he later became Miami's head coach.

In the meantime, I filled a staff vacancy by hiring one of our former quarterbacks, Houston Nutt, away from Arkansas State. I remember calling Arkansas State's head coach, Larry Lacewell, to

Defensive coordinator Pat Jones became Oklahoma State's head coach from 1984 to 1994. Photo courtesy of Oklahoma State University

tell him what I wanted to do. Larry asked if there was any way I could avoid hiring Nutt, but I said this was a guy I had to have. And Larry understood. He wasn't mad at me.

When Butch left, that opened up the receiver job for Nutt. I had one assistant left to hire and that's when I got Kevin Steele. I had run into Kevin that spring when he was working at New Mexico State. He was sharp and he hustled. We met him in the Dallas area and had some drinks with some of the other fellows down there. I was pretty impressed with the guy. I thought he had a lot on the ball. Baylor must have thought so, too. Kevin got hired as Baylor's head coach a few years later.

INSIDE INFO

There's a reason I didn't mention Tony Wise in the staff changeover. Wise had left earlier to go to Syracuse, but that wasn't his first offer.

We were scheduled to play Arizona State in the 1984 opener and we devoted a segment of spring practice to prepare for that game. We had even gone out to Arizona to talk with Larry Smith and the University of Arizona staff about Arizona State. We were playing somebody they were scheduled to play, so we shared information, which is not uncommon. Everybody does that.

Right after spring drills, Arizona State's coach, Darryl Rogers, called Jimmy and wanted permission to talk to Tony Wise. Darryl wanted to hire an offensive line coach.

Tony basically wanted Jimmy's OK to go out there and look around. Jimmy pretty much blew a fuse. Why? We've got the opener with Arizona State and have already practiced for them, so it looks like they are trying to get inside information on what we plan to do against them. I can't remember what was said or how it was said, but it wasn't real pleasant.

I don't blame Jimmy. I felt sorry for Tony, but I understood Jimmy's side of it, too. After that, about the time we started spring recruiting, Syracuse called about Tony. Dick MacPherson wanted to hire Tony, but Tony was a little taken aback by how Jimmy reacted to the Arizona State deal. Jimmy bowed up pretty good and I think it scared Tony a bit. Tony is about as non-confrontational as any guy who has ever lived. That's just his nature.

Tony knew somebody up there at Syracuse and instantly took the Syracuse job when it was offered. To take Tony's place, we hired Brad Seely, the offensive line coach and assistant head coach at the University of Pacific. Brad has gone on to a fine career and is still coaching in the NFL.

LAST WORDS

I would be remiss if I didn't mention in this book what Jimmy Johnson means to me.

When people talk about loyalty, sometimes it's just a word. But to me, loyalty is a two-way street. And the first thing that pops into my mind when I think of loyalty is Jimmy Johnson.

I tell this story when I really want people to know what Jimmy is all about.

In 1976, I left Arkansas to take a job at SMU. Well, I got a call in Dallas that my father was in the hospital in Little Rock and had been diagnosed with lung cancer. I was told I had better get up there.

By the time I got to Little Rock, the first guy I saw at the hospital was Jimmy Johnson. He beat me there.

My father didn't die that day. He died several months later. Basically, they opened him up and closed him up and said, "Good luck, Mr. Jones." In those days, that was all they could do.

But the first person to get to my father's bedside was Jimmy Johnson. My father was always very fond of him. That's a side of Jimmy I don't believe people really think about at all. The guy was immensely loyal. To this day, I would probably take a bullet for him.

CHAPTER 8

Run for the National Title

1984

BOWL BONUS

There was a big fringe benefit to playing in the 1983 Bluebonnet Bowl. A Houston-area kid named Thurman Thomas hung around our practices almost every day because he was enamored with No. 34, Ernest Anderson.

Thurman wore No. 34, just like Ernest, and they were about the same stature. Thurman knew Ernest had led the nation in rushing in '82. We practiced all the time in the dome before that bowl, and Thurman and his dad were around a lot. You could do that sort of thing back then. And you could tell Thurman wanted to like Oklahoma State.

Butch Davis and Willie Anderson did a good job recruiting Thurman. After our Bluebonnet Bowl win, George Walstad and I drove to Dallas to recruit and decided to call some of our buddies for sideline passes to the Cotton Bowl, where Texas was playing Georgia.

The Georgia and Texas coaches were congratulating us for what we had done that season and Ken Dabbs, Texas' recruiting coordinator, let me in on a pleasant surprise. Ken told me we were going to get Thurman Thomas.

Ken was upset at his people, because Texas tried to recruit Thurman as a cornerback.

Thurman was not held in quite the same esteem as Earl Campbell or Billy Sims or Eric Dickerson, but he was generally considered the best back in Texas during his senior year. He wasn't supposed to be that super, super player, but he was a very highly sought-after guy. And Ken told me we were going to get the kid because Thurman liked Ernest, he liked what we were doing offensively, and he knew he was going to get the ball if he played for us.

Thurman had a group called "the council" to help him decide where to go. The council consisted of his family members, and whoever recruited Thurman had to meet with them. They asked us to draw up our No. 1 running play. Ernest had led the country in rushing with a classic power play. Anyhow, the meeting with our coaches and the council went well.

HUSH HUSH

Thurman Thomas committed to us and ran for more yards (4,595) than any player in OSU history. He was also a great NFL back, playing in four Super Bowls with the Buffalo Bills and earning a spot in the Pro Football Hall of Fame.

When Thurman committed, we wanted him to keep it a secret and take other recruiting visits. It was pretty smart of Butch or Willie or whoever came up with this idea, because we didn't want everybody drilling him about it.

Word never leaked out that we had Thurman in the fold until about a week before signing day. At the same time, I was recruiting Curtis Luper, a kid from Sherman, Texas, who was generally considered the second-best running back in Texas that year. We were afraid if news got out that Thurman or Curtis had committed, other schools would try to use one against the other and try to talk them out of coming.

I was upfront with Curtis and told him we were going to get Thurman. Curtis was a cousin of Chris Rockins, who had been a heck of a defensive back for us. We knew we were going to get Curtis, but I warned him somebody would try to use Thurman against him. R.C. Slocum was the assistant recruiting Curtis for Texas A&M. He tried to do exactly that. We signed both kids without a hitch, and now Curtis is OSU's running backs coach.

ONE THAT GOT AWAY

We stockpiled some real offensive weapons over the next few years. We also thought we were going to get a quarterback from Henryetta, Oklahoma, that everyone wanted.

We were under the impression that Troy Aikman was committed to us and was coming to OSU. He said he still had to make a visit to OU, where his girlfriend was, but told us not to worry about it. He went down there and the rest is history in that regard. We could have had Troy Aikman, Thurman Thomas, and Barry Sanders all at the same time. That's a Pro Football Hall of Fame backfield.

If Aikman had come to OSU, it probably would have prevented Mike Gundy from starting for a couple of years, but we would have had that bunch together with Hart Lee Dykes for a few seasons. We could have really had some firepower there.

BIG OPENER

We knew we were going to be good in 1984, my first season as head coach. How good, we didn't know. But we knew we would get a pretty accurate measuring stick when we opened the season at Arizona State, which had been picked No. 1 in preseason by *Sport* magazine and ranked 12th in the Associated Press poll.

Arizona State was loaded. The Sun Devils returned 21 starters from a team that led the Pac-10 in total offense and total defense the year before.

Oklahoma State beat Arizona State 45-3 in a 1984 opener, launching a Big Eight Coach of the Year season for first-year head coach Pat Jones.
Photo courtesy of Oklahoma State University

A funny thing happened before we played them. I was smoking a cigarette outside a little entrance to the locker rooms. Arizona State's coach, Darryl Rogers, walked up. Darryl had been a coach at Michigan State and was a guy of note. I knew that he didn't know me, but I was just going to see if he said anything. Finally, I introduced myself. "Hi, I'm Pat Jones."

Darryl acted like he knew me, but he didn't know me from Adam. We beat them 45-3 and, after the game when I went to shake hands with him at midfield, his face was white as a ghost.

SMASHING DEBUT

In the press conference following the Arizona State game, a sportswriter who I think was from the west coast asked me if I would rank it as the biggest win of my career. I said it was the first game of my career. He acted like he knew that and wrote it down, but he didn't know it.

The whole scene caught them off guard. Obviously, Arizona State knew we had a good football team, but they didn't know how good we were. They knew Jimmy Johnson had left, but Jimmy wasn't a household name at that time. By the time we left town, they knew who we were and how good we were.

We outgained Arizona State 475 yards to 212. Charles Crawford, a secret weapon for us after he had a big spring, ran for 137 yards.

The play that really started the avalanche came when Leslie O'Neal hit their quarterback, Jeff Van Raaphorst, and the ball flew up in the air. Rodney Harding caught it and ran it in for a touchdown. We scored the first 23 points and the rout was on. They couldn't move the ball on us and they couldn't tackle Crawford. We put Crawford in maybe the second or third series and he literally ran wild on them. The zone play was big, because they were prepared for power and we ran zone schemes that Seely had brought when we hired him. We had it going pretty good. About halfway through the third quarter, maybe, I remember the public address guy asking all traffic officers to please man their stations. I looked around and folks were filing out of there. We were all business prior to the game. We were ready to play and we flat annihilated a nationally ranked team.

STAYING HUMBLE

We were unranked entering the 1984 season, but we jumped all the way to No. 13 after we beat Arizona State.

The guys who had been on our staff for a while still remembered the "knock your eyes out" statement that came back to haunt us in 1980, so we wanted to make sure we did not get big heads. We shut off media access to players about a day early to help in that regard.

Because the Arizona State game was played so late on a Saturday night, the score was not carried in Sunday newspapers in some time zones. Because of that, the national media didn't even seem to begin calling big-time until Tuesday.

To complicate things, we were late getting back from the trip, which made it a short week in terms of preparation. But we went out and had tough, physical workouts and beat Bowling Green 31-14 at home.

We didn't play very well and they lurked near us, but we intercepted four passes, and Mark Moore and Rod Brown each took one back for touchdowns. I was irritated and said after the game I would have to learn how to enjoy those kinds of wins.

ELITE COMPANY

We beat San Diego State 19-16 in our third game and moved into the top 10 of the AP poll for the first time since 1945.

We had legit worries before playing San Diego State. We lost 35-6 out there in 1982 and 23-16 against them at home in 1981. Our concerns were justified. They were driving downfield late in the game and, on a second-and-goal play, Mark Moore stripped the ball from one of their players at the one-yard line. Jim Krebs recovered with 1:38 left and we gave ourselves some breathing room a bit later when Seely suggested to me that we take an intentional safety by snapping the ball out of the end zone. They tried a Music City Miracle play at the end, but didn't get past the 30.

San Diego State's defensive coordinator was a guy I had coached with at SMU, Bernie Miller, who also had coached in the NFL. I had a great deal of respect for him. Bernie really was a good football coach and they played us about as well as anybody did, to be honest about it. But they couldn't get any offense against us, finishing with 196 total yards and minus-10 rushing yards.

MAKING AMENDS

Shawn Jones ran for 98 yards against San Diego State, but he also fumbled three times and we lost two of them. I told Shawn I wouldn't play a tailback who fumbled.

Shawn ran for 174 yards in a 31-7 win at Tulsa the next week. I gave him a game ball because I had given him so much heck about his fumbles. Thurman Thomas, our prize freshman, ran for a touchdown and threw a halfback pass to Jamie Harris for a score.

Quite a bit of buzz surrounded us when we went over to Tulsa. We were in the top 10 and it was announced before the game that we would play Nebraska on national television the following week. There was always a buzz when OSU came to Tulsa, but that added to it and we had a full house.

Jimmy liked to throw barbs at Tulsa and their coach, John Cooper, but I took the total opposite approach. They were well coached and Jimmy knew they were well coached, but he liked to dig at John a little and Cooper threw some back.

We held Rodney Harding out of that game. It might have been the only time that season that one of our defensive regulars missed a start. But we got after them pretty good and I recall that one of our guys even broke the jaw of Tulsa's quarterback, Steve Gage, a player we respected.

NICE WORK

At that point in the season, Rusty Hilger was completing 55 percent of his passes.

Rusty went on to play in the NFL. I mentioned earlier that he was the last kid we gave a scholarship to in 1979 and he was probably more skilled than we gave him credit for, but he still wasn't an eye-popping talent.

Rusty, God bless him, could be a bit of a loose cannon and could be a little wild at times. He had some daredevil in him. I remember during two-a-days or something, he had fallen out of the back of a car. The other coaches kept that information from me and they didn't let him throw. But Larry Coker and the offensive coaches did one of the best coaching jobs with that kid that I have ever seen.

CLARIFICATION NEEDED

Nebraska and OSU were both ranked in the top 10 when we played a national TV game in 1984. Keith Jackson and Frank Broyles were there for the TV crew. It was a big deal and a big ballgame.

We knew we had a chance to beat them and we were playing well. It was a great game with a great atmosphere in Lincoln. We were ahead 3-0 at the half when the sideline reporter, Tim Brant, stuck a microphone in my face and asked something to the extent of, "What are you going to tell your guys at halftime?"

I said something like, "I'm going to tell them to do whatever we've got to do to win. Maybe we'll win 3-0 or maybe we've got to try to outscore them."

We lost the game 17-3 and, because of that halftime interview, people thought I wanted to sit on the lead and try to win 3-0. I still get asked about that to this day on call-in shows. I have tried to explain myself, but apparently I haven't done a very good job.

This is the truth: We did want to establish the run, but we weren't afraid to do whatever we had to do to win the game. We threw the ball 28 times and probably called a few more in which we pulled the ball down and took off running or something. We threw for 242 yards. That was just a case of an out-of-control sound bite. It painted a very erroneous picture and got blown out of proportion.

The score was 3-3 going into the fourth quarter. We got bottled up and Shane Swanson ran a punt back 49 yards to put Nebraska ahead with about nine minutes left. They got another late score when they caught us blitzing and hit a slant pattern.

Keep in mind that we had a touchdown negated by penalty and we threw an interception in the end zone. Essentially, it was an even ballgame and we got beat 17-3 on a special teams touchdown. They still hadn't scored a rushing touchdown on us in two years because we had a combination of blitzes that messed them up. In 1983 and 1984, the Cornhuskers scored three offensive touchdowns against us.

LESSON FROM BEAR

Criticism went from one extreme to the other. The following week, people accused me of running up the score in a 47-10 win over Kansas. Rusty Hilger and Ronnie Williams, who we let throw, combined to hit 19-of-25 passes and Ken Zachary had four touches for 95 yards.

I'm not a big proponent of running up the score and I witnessed first-hand that a coach can take measures to keep from embarrassing an opponent. We played Alabama when I was at SMU and, after the Crimson Tide built a big lead, Bear Bryant instructed his team to punt on third down. Don't believe it when a coach says there is no way he can keep the score down.

Rusty Hilger of Southeast High School in Oklahoma City led the Cowboys to Bluebonnet Bowl and Gator Bowl wins in 1983 and 1984 en route to the NFL. *Photo courtesy of Oklahoma State University*

BIG MEN ON CAMPUS

Homecoming is always a big deal at OSU. Usually, we let our players walk around to see all the floats and homecoming houses. A huge buzz had generated about us because of the way we had been playing. We got a big kick out of it, because people hollered wherever we walked.

We went to a pep rally at Lewis Field, and when we walked down that ramp, I bet you one whole side of that stadium was full. There had to be at least 20,000 people in there. Even with the buzz going on, that took us aback a little bit. Things were really popping and it was an extremely exciting time to be a Cowboy.

We were still in the top 10 even though we had lost to Nebraska. We played Colorado in a homecoming game and beat them 20-14. I remember sweating it out because the score was closer than it needed to be thanks to four fumbles—including two near the goal line.

We clinched it when John Washington sacked Colorado quarterback Steve Vogel, the same guy who led a comeback against us in 1981, on a fourth-down play with 24 seconds left.

THURMAN BREAKS OUT

We got our first real sign of what Thurman Thomas was all about in a 34-6 win over Kansas State. Thurman entered the game on our third series, finishing with 206 yards and two touchdowns on 34 carries.

It was debated when we should start him. We were giving him more and more carries, but we had Charlie Crawford and we had Shawn Jones. We knew Thurman was good and we wanted to get him more and more work. That was a game where we were able to do it.

MOVING ON UP

We continued to win and people ranked ahead of us fell by the wayside. We were on course for the most high-stakes Bedlam game in history, but we didn't want to overlook anyone on the way.

We beat Missouri 31-13 under temporary lights—it was one of ESPN's early night games—and we scored on consecutive possessions after Leslie O'Neal blocked a field goal attempt that could have cut our lead to 17-16.

Then, on a cold and rainy day in Stillwater, we held on to beat Iowa State 16-10. The Cyclones had a fourth-and-15 at our 27 at the end of the game and Windell Yancy knocked down a pass intended for Tracy Henderson at the 10. Yancy paid dividends for the OSU basketball program later. One of his relatives, Terrel Harris, became a Cowboy basketball player.

NO. 2 VS. NO. 3

We were given a lot of national media attention in the month leading up to the Oklahoma game. *The New York Times* did a big spread on us. *Sports Illustrated* had been down to Stillwater. The bowl people were all over us.

Leading into this Bedlam ballgame, all those things were happening. It was just a totally magical time for everybody, and the kids were handling the pressure great even though there was a lot of hype—and justifiably so, because this was the biggest Bedlam game ever played.

We were ranked No. 2 and OU was ranked No. 3 in the UPI poll. The rankings were reversed in the AP poll. Basically, we were in a two-game playoff for the national championship.

The winner of the Bedlam game was going to go to the Orange Bowl to plead a case for the national title. That was the year BYU would win the national championship, going unbeaten and defeating a 6-5 Michigan team in the Holiday Bowl.

We knew this was high-stakes stuff when we went down to Norman on the bus. Our approach was to just go down there and kick the door in. The bus ride was almost like a presidential caravan. Cars were honking and everything.

PREGAME TIDBITS

Coaches always meet with the TV crew before a televised game so the broadcasters can get a little insight. We were a little bit less than truthful with Coach Broyles, the color analyst, because we were doing some stuff against Oklahoma's wishbone that I didn't want to tell him. Later on I apologized, but we didn't want to divulge our defensive game plan to anybody.

That was my first time at OU as a head coach. I was standing outside the dressing room pretty early before the game and not many people were around. Nobody was belligerent to us or anything.

A middle-aged guy with a nice-looking kid stood over where I was smoking a cigarette. They had their red gear on and I could tell they were looking at me, so I walked over and introduced myself. The guy said he didn't want to bother me, but the kid really wanted my autograph. And he had on all of his OU stuff. They were OU people. The dad said he could not thank me enough. That always stuck with me, because I never really did get wrapped up into the Bedlam rivalry a great deal. I was struck by the respect the OU folks had for us and for our football team.

MAIN EVENT

The biggest Bedlam game ever played was a pretty even contest. We scored a touchdown right before the half. The clock was about to run out before we scored and I don't recall us having any timeouts left. The OU players were slow lining up because they wanted time to expire. Referee John McClintock, who later became the Big Eight's director of officials, got in there to stop the clock with four seconds left, and Rusty Hilger threw a fade to Jamie Harris for a touchdown to tie the score at 7-7.

OU's coach, Barry Switzer, ran down John when the half ended and got after him pretty good. I remember going by, slapping John on the rear, and saying, "Nice call, good job" because I didn't want Barry to intimidate him too much.

Early in the second half, Rusty Hilger dropped a snap, picked it up, and threw a 77-yard touchdown pass to Malcolm Lewis to give us a 14-7 lead.

Andy Dillard and Scott Verplank, two pro golfers who played at OSU, were on the sideline with us. I want to say Dillard had a Boston Bruins jersey on, but when Hilger hit that throw, I remember seeing Dillard turn around to the OU crowd and unload with both middle fingers. I told him to quit it, because I didn't want to make those people any madder than they already were.

OU scored 10 points to go up 17-14 entering the fourth quarter and it looked like we were going to get the ball for a chance to make a drive and win the game. Bobby Riley fumbled a fair catch and OU recovered at our 25, setting up a 20-yard Spencer Tillman touchdown run. That was the last score of the game and OU won 24-14.

Coach Broyles asked me later why I didn't go out and complain to the officials that Riley had been interfered with while trying to catch the punt. But what good does it do to complain about a call? I wasn't into whining about calls. They called it and I wasn't going to talk them out of it. I didn't complain about it after the game, either. I didn't want the whole thing to come across as, "The Aggies are griping about being cheated." That was just a high-stakes game that we didn't win.

WHOLE NEW BALLGAME

I really thought that game took the Bedlam rivalry to another level. I thought it changed the complexion of the event even though we didn't win. It was the only game on national television that day. The whole deal was as big as it could literally get. It was the last game of the regular season and the only way it could have been bigger would have been if we were ranked Nos. 1-2 instead of Nos. 2-3.

I thought everybody showed respect. I can't remember anybody showing any hatred. It was competitive. They knew we had a good football team. From that game on, I think Bedlam took a little bit different tone.

OSU beat OU in 1976 and we should have won that 21-20 game against them in 1983, but this was a classic high-stakes, end-of-the-season matchup. Even though we didn't win, I thought it almost erased the "poor Aggie" concept. We had a very good football team. We were ranked high. Even though we were not going to the Orange Bowl, we were going to the Gator Bowl. We still had a pretty good sense of accomplishment.

GATOR HUNT

The Gator Bowl people were ecstatic over landing two top-10 teams. We were No. 9 and South Carolina was No. 7. Plus, South Carolina was going to bring about a jillion fans and our people were excited to go to Florida. Coincidentally, we stayed at the Sea Turtle Inn on Jacksonville Beach. That was the same place I had gone to accept a job at Pitt a few years earlier.

Before the Gator Bowl, I flew to New York with Pat Quinn, our sports information director, so we could attend a promotional deal for the bowl staged by ABC. South Carolina's head coach, Joe Morrison, was there, too.

We were staying right off Central Park and ABC was playing it up as Joe Morrison's return to New York. Joe was a big-name guy up there because he had been with the New York Giants.

Head coach Pat Jones and ABC's Lynn Swann meet during pregame warm-ups at the Gator Bowl. *Photo courtesy of Oklahoma State University*

They brought back a bunch of his old teammates, including Sam Huff and Fran Tarkenton. It was a who's who of all the Giants I had watched as a youngster, so they were larger than life to me.

I was a first-year head coach, so they didn't know me from Adam. I didn't really know Joe Morrison, but I knew of him. We hadn't been at that function five minutes and they were all over Joe, making a big fuss about him. Joe came up to me and said something like, "As soon as this is over, we are going to the bar. I've got to get my butt out of here."

Joe did not like the attention. I think he felt a little bit awkward because they made a big deal over him and not us, even though I didn't feel slighted. But I gained a comrade out of that situation. Joe Morrison was a close friend until he died.

WILD RIDE

During our team's bus ride to the Gator Bowl, we became caught in traffic amid the South Carolina crowd. It got a little crazy. They weren't rocking our bus, but they were damn close and a lot of words were directed at our players. They said some things that weren't real nice to some of our black kids. It got very quiet, and either Rodney Harding or one of our coaches said, "We've got them right where we want them." That lightened up the mood and off we went.

AGGIE MAGIC

I allowed myself to be wired for a heart monitor and sound at the Gator Bowl. ABC thought that was neat.

So many Gamecock people were in the stands that it was almost a South Carolina home game, but we had a lot of people there, too. The game set an attendance record of more than 82,000, and it was the largest crowd ever to watch OSU play football.

We had the best team. I knew that when the game started. We scored the first 13 points, but they caught up with us and

OSU players and coaches celebrate a 21-14 Gator Bowl victory over South Carolina that clinched the first 10-win season in school history.
Photo courtesy of Oklahoma State University

went ahead by a point. We had to score on our last drive, which started at our 12, and I told Larry Coker that it was four-down territory all the way.

We started dinking and dunking and got it across midfield, converting a fourth-and-six along the way. We were in field goal range. I told Larry, "Go ahead, let's try to keep going." We hit Barry Hanna on a crossing route. They busted a coverage. We were hollering for Hanna to get out of bounds so the clock would stop. We thought he got knocked out of bounds, but he didn't. Bang, he made a great run down the sideline, bouncing off a couple of guys, and went in for a 25-yard touchdown reception with about a minute left. It was Hanna's only touchdown that season. We went for two and won the game, 21-14.

Thurman Thomas ran for 155 yards and was MVP of the game. Leslie O'Neal and Rod Brown both were named All-Americans.

VICTORY LAP

The bus ride back to the hotel after the game was probably the most pleasurable hour that I have ever spent. Nobody else had ever won 10 games in a season at Oklahoma State, but we did it. We made a run at a national championship. We didn't accomplish that, but we knew we were going to finish in the top 10. It would have been a real injustice had that group of kids not finished in the top 10.

STOP, THIEF

The only bad thing about the Gator Bowl was that somebody stole my Aggie jersey. I had a jersey made before the start of the season that said "Oklahoma Aggies" sprawled across the front.

That jersey might have offended some of the younger folks, but I had seen a picture of Mr. Iba wearing gear that said Oklahoma Aggies. Champion was our knitwear company, so I called and asked them to make me one. I asked Mr. Iba if he thought anyone would care if I wore one of those jerseys. He told me, "Damn it, get that jersey made and wear it!" so that's what I did. It created a bit of a buzz, but it was a throwback to the old Aggies. I never found out who took my Aggie jersey.

CHAPTER 9

Thurman Breaks Through

1985

SUPER RECRUITS

We finished fifth in the UPI poll and seventh in the AP poll in 1984, putting us in position to pursue high-caliber recruits. Among our 27 signees in 1985 were two *Parade* All-Americans, Hart Lee Dykes and Melvin Gilliam.

Hart Lee was *USA Today*'s offensive player of the year. Of course his recruitment, which has been well documented, put us and a few other schools on probation.

I had concerns about that deal all along. The funny thing about it is he never made an official recruiting visit, although people forget—and I don't know whether we ever made an issue out of it—he actually was on our campus.

Hart Lee had a brother up at Phillips University in Enid named Todd Chambers. Todd was a scholarship basketball player at OU and transferred to Phillips.

Our coaches knew about Hart Lee's brother. They knew Hart was making a trip up there over the course of the summer to see his brother, so they had Hart stop off in Stillwater on his way to Enid. Hart came by and met us. So he had been on our campus. It wasn't like we signed him sight unseen.

Knowing the area he was from—Bay City, Texas—and the caliber of athlete he was, my experience told me something would probably come down on the guy one way or another in regard to a rules violation or cheating or whatever you want to call it.

In that part of Texas, when you were dealing with that magnitude of player, historically that's the way it went down. Everybody had a dog in the race. Everybody. That's the way it had been for decades for a guy of his caliber. I was worried we had done something to get him, although I never put pressure on any of our coaches. I just told them to go as hard as they could, to be smart, and not to get into trouble. If that's not good enough, it's not good enough.

One time late in the recruiting process, we thought we had lost him. I can't remember who I thought we were going to lose him to or exactly what happened, but I remember taking his name down off of the board. It wasn't like, "Oh my god, we've lost him! You guys do whatever you have got to do to get him!" That wasn't it. I think some people assume that was the case.

RARE BREED

Hart Lee Dykes was one of the finest big athletes with hand-eye coordination I have ever seen. I think he won the national punt, pass, and kick competition and the national pitch, hit, and throw competition in the same year when he was nine or 10 years old.

And he was smart. We never had a moment's problem with him over grades. He could have made straight A's if he wanted to. He was always a solid B student.

Dykes was also competitive, which helped us bring out the best in him. You had to stay on him in practice a little bit because

---

Hart Lee Dykes of Bay City, Texas, was an All-American in 1988 and is the leading receiver in Big Eight history. He was a first-round pick of the New England Patriots. *Photo courtesy of Oklahoma State University*

he was a man among boys. You had to make it competitive. When you made it competitive, he worked hard. He was no dog.

After his playing career, aside from the violations, no one could say he made a mistake in going to Oklahoma State. He ended up being the all-time leading receiver in the history of the Big Eight.

When we recruited him, the perception was we were a running football team. People were telling him that. Why would he go to Oklahoma State?

But his career, football-wise and educationally, worked out just fine for him. He was a first-team All-American and a three-time All-Big Eight wideout. He set records and became a first-round NFL draft pick.

If he hadn't torn up a knee in the NFL, I think he would have played in the pros for a long time. I think he would have been remembered as one of the outstanding big receivers in the history of the league. I think he was that supreme of an athlete. He was 6-foot-4 and 222 pounds and ran as fast as he wanted to. People questioned his speed, but guys couldn't catch him. I don't know what his vertical jump was, but he could leap out of the gym. He could throw a 100 mph fastball. This guy was a physical freak. He was really what we were looking for.

To me, it's a tragedy that this NCAA stuff came down on him. I'm not trying to take any blame off anybody, but on the same hand, this was neither the first nor the last time that it occurred with a recruit of his level down in that area of Texas. If you started naming high-caliber athletes over the years who were involved in something like this, all of us would probably be taken aback a bit. A good number of schools never received sanctions for it, but that's just the way it was.

STRONG-ARM TACTICS

We returned 15 starters in 1985, but were a little bit concerned because we were going to have to break in a new starting quarterback in a season opener at Washington.

Ronnie Williams, a sophomore, was going to be our guy. Paul Jette had signed Ronnie out of Wichita Falls, Texas, the year before. That was a pretty good coup, because we had to get a quarterback and Ronnie was highly recruited.

Ronnie had played enough behind Rusty Hilger and had tasted enough big-time success that we felt he was ready to go. Ronnie had a big arm. He was a little bit slow-footed, but he was a big, imposing guy, commanded a lot of respect, and was very highly regarded within the squad.

Ronnie ended up losing his job the next season when Mike Gundy came along, but Ronnie might have had the strongest arm I have seen. He probably could wow you with arm strength as much as anybody I had ever been around, including Dan Marino. He didn't have the touch that some others did, but he was a competitive guy and a good leader.

FEVER PITCH

Anticipation for the 1985 season was probably as big as any time in the program's history. We were coming off consecutive bowl victories, and Thurman Thomas had been named the AP's offensive newcomer of the year the season before.

The future looked bright, and it wasn't just because we had installed permanent lights at Lewis Field. It was a period when everybody associated with the program felt good about himself.

Another reason everyone was excited was because we were going to play a nationally televised season opener at Washington, a team that had just beaten OU in the Orange Bowl. *Sports Illustrated* picked Washington No. 1 in its preseason issue. The Huskies got two first-place votes in the AP poll and were ranked 12th.

We had to play them with two new cornerbacks, but our defensive backfield was in good hands. We had hired Louis Campbell to be our defensive coordinator and coach the secondary after Paul Jette left us. Louis was an Arkansas guy. I had known Louis for a long time and we had coached together at SMU. Louis was the secondary coach at Alabama for Bear Bryant. But Louis wanted to be a coordinator and we hired him.

THEY CAN'T TACKLE THURMAN

We knew Washington was a live place. We had talked to other people about that stadium. There is actually a moat around it. You go under the moat and then come out on the other side. Some schools had issues up there because Washington would try to intimidate teams in the tunnel.

They had a great crowd. They hit a throw on us early and we got behind, but they couldn't stop Thurman Thomas. Thurman ran 40 times for 237 yards, and we beat them 31-17. At the time, USC's Charles White was the only player ever to run for more yards against Washington.

It was a huge win, and we had become a program that was used to winning big games. It was the second year in a row that we won an opener against a team that a national publication had picked to win the national championship.

I used my postgame press conference to suggest that Thurman should be a candidate for the Heisman Trophy. Never mind that he was a true sophomore. I had enough sense to realize it was a nationally televised game and, if I said that, it would set the stage for him. And he had a legitimate Heisman-type performance.

JAWBREAKER

The bad news was that we lost our new starting quarterback in the Washington game. They hit Ronnie Williams and broke his jaw in the third quarter.

The score was tied at 17 when Rusty Rankin came off the bench to lead a go-ahead scoring drive. Mark Moore clinched the game with an interception return for a touchdown.

Rusty, a third-year sophomore from Vinita, Oklahoma, was a heck of a smart guy, but he was not unusually talented and had not played much before. I told our offensive coordinator, Larry Coker, not to call a pass unless he cleared it with me first, because Washington couldn't tackle Thurman.

I remember Larry asking me if I cared if we threw a halfback pass. Thurman threw a touchdown pass to Bobby Riley. But we didn't need to throw because we were gnawing them up running the ball.

When Ronnie's jaw got broken, it was not a cheap shot. One of their players hit him right underneath his facemask. But the deal got more interesting about a week later. My secretary, Joyce Robbins, got a phone call and told me this was one I might want to take.

A guy was calling from Oregon or somewhere out on the west coast. He told me he wasn't a crackpot. He said he was a doctor who had been tracking a trend for a good number of years in the Pac-10.

He read off a string of quarterbacks who had their jaws broken when playing Washington. It was a pretty extensive list with four or five recognizable names.

He said, "Coach, just to let you know, your quarterback is not the first guy this has happened to. I'm not saying they are cheating. I'm not saying they are doing anything, but I have seen this go on and I just wanted to share this with you."

I don't know what his motivation was. I just think he thought they were cheap-shotting quarterbacks. They were a rough group, but we were too. The hit on him wasn't a late hit. Their guy just came up and busted him under the chin. After that, I made all our quarterbacks wear a big facemask cage that came down in front.

FAMILY BUSINESS

I was a little irritated after the Washington game. I thought they hit Thurman a couple of times over in their bench area and the officiating crew came close to letting the game get out of hand.

The Pac-10 provided the crew, so I called the director of Pac-10 officials. I told him I had never really done this and I was not one to argue about calls, but I thought he should know that the crew almost let the game get out of control.

He very nicely told me he was going to take exception with me because the referee was his son. I looked at the referee's name and it was Jim Springer. And the head official's name was Jim Springer. I didn't have enough sense to put two and two together.

But I told him Washington couldn't tackle Thurman, and I really thought they got after him pretty good over there in the bench area. We were lucky we didn't have a real melee going on, because we had some guys who wouldn't take one iota off anybody—Thurman included.

TIME FOR MOURNING

We were afraid of a letdown after the big win against Washington and we barely beat North Texas 10-9 in a home opener. They played us better than Washington did, quite honestly.

But that's not adversity. Real adversity came immediately after that. One of our first-year freshmen, a defensive lineman named James Clark, committed suicide in his dorm room.

Brad Dennis, one of our kickers, called over to the football office to tell us about it. The secretary came to get us and told us Brad was just as rattled as he could be. He said something real bad had happened and we needed to get over there as fast as we could.

George Walstad and I got over to the dorm just about the time paramedics were bringing out the body. Our freshmen were all living on the same floor of the high-rise dorm. Those guys were in a pretty good state of shock.

George had signed James Clark out of Wilmer-Hutchins in South Dallas. We went back to the office and we called his high school coach. I didn't know the kid's family. His mother worked at some kind of discount store down there. We told the high school coach what had happened and had him go down to the store. We wanted somebody to be there when she heard the news. I think he spoke to the store management just to let them know what was going on.

His mother wouldn't have known my voice from Adam, but George knew her. I didn't want to be a total stranger calling her to tell her the bad news, so I asked George to do it. He agreed to make the call.

George tried to break the news to her as gently as possible, but then he held the phone away from his head and I could hear her screaming. I was watching George and I was then concerned about him. That's why I had gotten Leslie O'Neal and one of the other defensive linemen to come provide moral support for George. I told them I hated to ask them this, but it was big-boy stuff and we needed them for George's sake.

George was an armed services veteran and an older guy, but this was a tough duty. After it was all said and done, George put the phone down and took a real deep breath. I remember O'Neal and whoever the other kid was went over there and grabbed hold of George. They put their arms around him just to say, "Hey Coach, it's OK, we're all here."

We didn't really have anybody who served as a team chaplain, but I got Jim Struthers from the Presbyterian Church to talk to our players. He gave a nice service or memorial. I also called some of my buddies in psychology and university services to request counselors. We had some of those folks come around for the freshmen or anybody else—even the coaches—if they needed to talk to them.

When people speak about the strength and leadership and internal workings of a football team, I still think back to those kids and George. The leadership of that squad, those upperclassmen, they watched after the freshmen. The right stuff was occurring. Everything else got to be secondary, but we were concerned with some of those freshmen and what they had seen and the youngster who found him. I remember talking to a couple of the psychological people after the fact and the common theme with a suicide is, you can't figure these things out.

WIRED FOR ACTION

We had an open date to recover from the tragedy. We beat Miami of Ohio and Tulsa in our next two games, pitching our second and third second-half shutouts in improving our record to 4-0. Harry Roberts returned an interception for a touchdown and Thurman ran a punt back for a score in the Miami game.

The Tulsa game was notable because we got Ronnie Williams back. He returned to duty with five minutes left in the first quarter and, with his broken jaw wired shut, I'm still not sure how we called plays.

We needed Ronnie because Nebraska was coming in for a night game the next week. Even though we were ranked fifth and they were ranked ninth, the Cornhuskers were a five-point favorite.

We came back from a 20-3 deficit and lost 34-23, but Ronnie Williams produced one of the most heroic and courageous big-game performances I have ever been around. He set school records for completions and passing yards (363), and I think his jaw was still wired shut. This game was really Ronnie's coming-out party. He had a chance to be something pretty doggone good.

Ronnie Williams led OSU to the 1985 Gator Bowl and was a team captain when the Cowboys beat West Virginia in the 1987 Sun Bowl.
Photo courtesy of Oklahoma State University

LESLIE'S MONSTER GAME

Kansas was one of the nation's better offensive teams in 1985. The Jayhawks averaged 450 yards and 33.3 points. Their quarterback, Mike Norseth, was throwing for 326 yards a game. We beat them 17-10 because Thurman Thomas took a screen pass 30 yards to the two and scored a winning touchdown from the one with a minute left.

Norseth had only 16 completions and 197 passing yards because Leslie O'Neal had the kind of day defensive players dream about. He was chosen as the Big Eight's defensive player of the week because he had eight tackles, two sacks, three quarterback pressures, a forced fumble, a fumble recovery, and an interception.

There are not many games in which a defensive lineman shows up so much, but he was a Lombardi finalist that year and probably should have won it. He was a legitimate two-time All-American. Could anybody block him? No. And his foot speed and leverage were just a dream. Speed-wise, he probably was a little bit of a physical freak for a lineman. He was very gifted and a great worker.

ALTITUDE OR ATTITUDE?

Colorado had gone to a wishbone offense and ranked seventh nationally in rushing when we played them in '85. But Thurman Thomas ran for 201 yards and we won 14-11. Thurman popped a 60-yard touchdown run on the third play of the second half to put us up 14-3.

The game was played in Boulder. People ask me, "Did the altitude ever bother your players?" It didn't bother Thurman or Barry Sanders. That's what we always told our guys. Barry had big ballgames out there in later years. If you are the right person, altitude doesn't bother you.

Not much bothered Thurman in '85. By this point in the season, Thurman had 1,051 rushing yards in seven games.

FIGHTING BACK

One of our linebackers, Jim Krebs, made 26 tackles against Colorado. He should have made a lot of tackles for what we were doing gameplan-wise, and he went wild.

Krebs was a tough guy. He came back from a broken arm and a knee injury. I had signed him out of junior college, and I am not so sure that at one point in time I didn't tell him, "I don't know whether you ought to play football anymore." He was just so tough and he wanted to play. It was meaningful to him.

MOON OVER MANHATTAN

Kansas State fired Jimmy Dickey during the 1985 season. I really thought they made a mistake when he was let go.

Lee Moon, who I had known years before when he was an assisant football coach at Virginia, was an assistant athletic director at Kansas State and took over as the interim coach during the final nine games of the '85 season.

When we played K-State that season, he made a pregame remark to me about "how good it felt to be coaching again," or something like that.

We beat the dog out of them. Thurman ran for 213 yards and four touchdowns in a 35-3 blowout that could have been worse. I got a laugh after the game when Lee told me, "I just thought I wanted to do this again."

BOWLING AGAIN

We had travel problems getting to a game at Missouri. The weather became bad and we couldn't land in Columbia or St. Louis. We went to Kansas City, finally landed there, and took buses to Columbia. I had all I wanted of that.

The first guys I saw getting off the bus were the folks from the Gator Bowl, who I recognized since we had been there only the year before.

Well, the kids were hungry, and we were so far off schedule that I was out of sorts. One of the Gator Bowl guys said, "Coach, I just want to remind you that if you win tomorrow, the worst you are going to do is be back in our bowl again." That just made me even antsier, because we had to win the ball game. I knew what was at stake.

Missouri was only 1-8 before the game and we beat them 21-19, getting all three touchdowns, including a Harry Roberts interception return, in a two-minute span in the second quarter. Their kicker hit four field goals and missed three others, so we survived by the skin of our teeth.

We were 8-1 and my record as a head coach was 18-3, but what worried me were our near misses. We had won our last three road games by a combined total of 12 points and injuries were starting to take a toll, especially at receiver. I feared we were near the end of our streak.

ARCTIC BLAST

We were ranked seventh in the country when we went to Iowa State. I knew we weren't that good or as good as we were the year before, but, doggone, we had gotten to 8-1 and if we could get to 9-1, who knows what might happen in terms of staying in contention for championships?

Well, we got off the bus up there in Ames and it was the worst winter snowstorm you had ever seen. Snow, wind, cold—everything. This was way worse than the Ice Bowl game against OU the following week. People don't understand that because the OU game was nationally televised. But these weather conditions were incredibly bad, borderline call-off-the-game bad, which they weren't going to do.

When we got off that bus, our South Texas guys, including Thurman, the toughest human being I've ever been around, were wide-eyed. Boy, it was really freezing.

I still get cold thinking about the mustache of our offensive line coach, Brad Seely. When we first got out there, I remember looking up at Brad. His mustache was completely frozen and icicles were hanging down. I thought, "Oh, gosh, just let us win one more game and get out of here." We couldn't do it. They stormed the field, and Jim Criner got himself a huge win. That was a legit upset. I was afraid the law of averages was running out on us. I knew it. But if this game had been in Stillwater, we might have won it instead of losing 15-10.

We lost any shot for a Big Eight championship and accepted another Gator Bowl bid. It was a downer and we were disappointed, but I guess it showed just how far the program had come. As disappointed as we were, we were still in the dressing room accepting a bid to the Gator Bowl, which was a big deal. It's still a big deal.

THE ICE BOWL

The Bedlam games of this era were high-stakes contests. If we hadn't lost at Iowa State, we could have entered this game for the second year in a row as a legit contender in the national championship race. OU ended up winning the national championship that season.

Both of us were ranked in the top 20, and kickoff was moved to nighttime to accommodate ESPN. Initially, it was not too bad. It began lightning and thundering and sleeting, but it wasn't frigid cold. But it was getting colder and, by the time we came out to play the game, our field was pretty much a skating rink.

Even though he was running on a horrible track—you couldn't walk across that field—Thurman had one of the best performances I have ever seen against a very good OU defense. He became the first player to run for 100 yards against the Sooners that season.

OU won 13-0. They scratched out enough footing to hit a couple of field goals and our kicker, Brad Dennis, slipped down about twice when we had makeable field goal attempts. We were still firing away late in the game and I thought we could get a score, get an onside kick, and have a chance to win. I really thought it would come down to a possession game, but we could never hit a throw.

All kinds of lore and fables exist in regard to this game—things that occurred on and off the field. One story claims a lady couldn't get up to go to the restroom. She peed in her pants and it froze her to the seat. People were stranded and couldn't get back home. People were supposedly sledding down stadium aisles. I didn't see that stuff.

But it was almost like the Twilight Zone. We weren't freezing to death since we were bundled up, but it was surreal because of the lightning and ice and the covered field. Guys were slipping and sliding and trying to scratch footing into the ground.

I had a Corvette at the time and couldn't get my key in the door because the keyhole was covered with a layer of ice. I had someone douse the door with hot water so I could get the key into it. I wasn't concerned that the frozen Fiberglas might shatter if I threw hot water on it. I just wanted to go home, take a breath, and get away from it all, especially since I was being courted for a job opening at Pitt.

The Corvette handled terribly on the ice. It was a very weird night. Paul Maguire and Mike Patrick, who did the game for ESPN, always reminded me of it in later years when I saw them at NFL games. We had a snow game with Denver when I was coaching with the Raiders and Maguire said, "Here we go again."

GOODBYE PAT?

Before the Bedlam game, I got a call from a friend of mine, Bill Peckman, who was closely associated with the Pitt football program. Pitt was firing Foge Fazio, and Bill asked if I would be interested in becoming their next head coach. Bill said he was calling on behalf of their athletic director, Ed Bozik.

I told Bill I was interested, but I didn't want to deal with any of it until after the OU game. I also asked them to call my athletic director, Myron Roderick, to make sure everything was done above board.

WHIRLWIND TOUR

I had to fly to Jacksonville for a Gator Bowl press conference after the Ice Bowl. I fielded more questions about the Pitt job than I did about our bowl game against Florida State.

After I left I had to go to Houston for the Lombardi Award banquet. All this Pitt stuff was swirling around. I got a call from Paul Jette when I was staying at the Shamrock Hilton Hotel in Houston. Paul, who had left us to go to Miami with Jimmy Johnson, said he was being offered the defensive coordinator job at Texas and he wanted my opinion. I remember telling him I didn't even know what I was doing because my head was completely spun. He took the job at Texas.

I accompanied Leslie O'Neal at the Lombardi banquet. We sat with Tony Casillas and his wife, who is a really nice person, Mike Ruth from Boston College, and whoever the other finalist was that year.

We were there at the head table and, because they were honoring her for something, the invited guest for the event was Dionne Warwick. I remember telling her how talented I thought she was and that I enjoyed her music. She was a very nice lady and I thought she was very attractive. I was probably as impressed sitting by Dionne Warwick as anything else that night.

But all this was such a blur for me. So much was happening at the same time and we had to get ready for the bowl with Florida State.

BEHIND CLOSED DOORS

Amid everything else, Ed Bozik called me and we had a clandestine meeting in Dallas at an airport hotel. I think we might have done this before I got to Houston for the Lombardi event.

We went to dinner down in the hotel restaurant. Somehow word leaked out about the meeting and a Pittsburgh TV crew showed up. Ed and I retreated to his room, we kicked our shoes off, and were up there drinking beer and talking. It was one of those formal-informal deals. Ed was a vice president at Pitt when I was up there and I had played golf with him several times. He was a good guy and I really liked him.

I went back to my room. Apparently the Pittsburgh TV crew wasn't the only group that found out about the clandestine meeting. There came a knock at my door. I opened it up and it was Jerry Moore, who has just been fired as head coach at Texas Tech. I have known him a long time, and there he was at my hotel room with his offensive coordinator, Rob Best. And I didn't think anybody knew where I was. That is how weird things were getting.

They asked to come in and wanted to know if I would hire them if I took the Pitt job. To this day, I still don't know how they knew I was there or how they found out.

I CAN'T WAIT

A pre-bowl press conference had been scheduled the following Monday in Stillwater. Meanwhile, all this Pitt stuff was brewing in the media.

Pitt wanted to bring me up there to look around, but the university president, Dr. Wesley Posvar, was over in Europe. They wanted Dr. Posvar back on campus before I went up there.

By that time, Myron had given me a new contract proposal to stay at OSU. It was quite a bit better than my old deal. In fact, it might have been a tad better than what Pitt was going to pay.

But I was genuinely interested in the Pitt job and not just from the flattery standpoint that somebody else was interested in me. I have always liked the hustle and bustle of the east, so it was appealing.

The end of the week rolled around and the bowl press conference in Stillwater was coming up soon. I knew I would have to mention what was going on during that press conference, so I sped up the process.

I knew Pitt wanted me to wait until Dr. Posvar got back, but I called them and told them I had to come check things out right away. I didn't want to mess up their timetable, but I just had to see how it all felt before things proceeded any further.

I didn't know whether they were going to offer me the job and I didn't know whether I would take the job, but I wanted to confirm in my mind what it would feel like. So I got on a plane and flew to Pittsburgh.

I met with some money people, had dinner with folks, and toured campus and the facilities, which were a little bit run down. But Ed told me what they were planning to do and I was becoming pretty intrigued.

Before I left, it wasn't like, "You've got the job." It was something like, "As far as I'm concerned, you are the guy." And they could not officially offer me a job until Dr. Posvar got back. I think he was coming back Sunday night, so I told Ed to call me Monday morning before my press conference. I had to walk into that press conference and tell those people something and, to be fair to OSU, I didn't want to string things out any longer.

THE VERDICT

I got home and I was messing around when I actually found my old Pitt travel bag from the time I was an assistant. I laid it out in the garage. I still didn't know what I was going to do. I really didn't.

Jimmy Johnson called me and asked if I wanted the Pitt job. I knew it was a good job. They didn't have the quality of players that Oklahoma State did right then, but I knew it was probably a better job in the long term and it was easier to win at Pitt. They were still an eastern independent. You've got Penn State to cope with, but you don't have OU and these other guys to fight.

This is the truth in regard to what happened that Monday morning.

I was worn down from the season and from traveling to Jacksonville, Dallas, Houston, and Pittsburgh. Everything was a total blur. And I told myself, "I just can't do this. Professionally it might be the best thing to do, but I can't do it." I just could not pull the trigger.

Ed had not called yet and I still didn't know what he was going to say. While I was waiting for the phone to ring, I took out a pencil and a yellow tablet and wrote, "I want to thank the University of Pittsburgh for its interest, but I think it's best for me to remain at Oklahoma State."

The phone rang. I picked it up and it was Ed Bozik. I said, "Ed, before you say anything to me, don't say a word. Here's what I need to say in this press conference. I don't want to put any heat on you or anything." And I read to him what I had just written.

Ed said, "Is there anything else I can ask you?"

I said, "No, don't. The only thing I'm going to tell you is that I think Mike Gottfried is a good man."

I knew Gottfried and I were in the running for the job. If somebody put a gun to my head, I couldn't say that Ed Bozik was going to tell me, "This job is yours if you want it," because I didn't let him say it.

So if somebody asked me if Pitt officially extended me that job, I couldn't say they did. I didn't want to know. I had my mind made up.

I still don't know what he was going to say. Foge Fazio called me later on and told me, "Hey, I thought this job was yours. What happened?" I told him the story.

WHAT IF?

Do I ever wonder what might have happened if I had taken the Pitt job? It has crossed my mind.

Pitt didn't have Thurman Thomas and didn't have Hart Lee Dykes. Even though Leslie O'Neal was graduating and Barry Sanders hadn't signed yet, we still had better players than they did. I think Pitt would have been a better job long term than Oklahoma State, but at that particular point in time Oklahoma State had better players.

I enjoyed Pittsburgh when I had been there before. There was a lure about it. I've second-guessed myself on that decision. Not a lot, but some.

It was really my only chance to take another head coaching job. At that time, we really weren't under NCAA investigation. People said a few things because we had Dykes. Rumors were beginning to build a little bit, but had that stuff been circulating already, Pitt wouldn't have tried to come after me.

By the time we got to winning big again, we were in the throes of an investigation and I was probably perceived as damaged goods in that regard. But I was one of the first coaches who decided to stay at OSU when another school made a run at me, and that was a big deal to the Oklahoma State people.

GATOR, AGAIN

After all this transpired, we still had a bowl game to play against Bobby Bowden and Florida State. Both of our teams were ranked in the top 20, but I worried that taking our guys to the Gator Bowl for a second straight year might be anticlimactic for them. We had tried unsuccessfully to get more bowls in the Big Eight's parlay mix before we lost to Iowa State.

When the worst you do is end up in the Gator Bowl, that's not all that bad. The Gator Bowl was the equivalent of what the Cotton Bowl is today. But my fears were justified. Going back was less exciting for our guys who had been there before, because

Thurman Thomas, the all-time leading rusher in OSU history, was a two-time All-American and was MVP of a Gator Bowl and a Sun Bowl.
Photo courtesy of Oklahoma State University

we went to the same gator farm, went to the same aircraft carrier, and stayed in the same place.

I was so worn down from everything when I got down there that I was sick as a dog for about half a week and basically couldn't do anything. I just took medicine, stayed in my room, went to practice, and went to the things I had to attend. And that was about all.

FORE SCORE

Scott Verplank, a former Cowboy golfer, showed up for the bowl and I introduced him to Bobby Bowden. Bobby is a good golfer and Scott had already won some tournaments, so I think Bobby got a bigger kick out of meeting Scott than vice versa.

Florida State suspended one of its starting receivers, Hasan Jones, for selling bowl tickets. His coaches were having trouble deciding which quarterback to start. They settled on a freshman, Chip Ferguson.

I remember standing around out there before the game watching the team warm up with Louis Campbell and some of our other coaches saying, "If this is Chip Ferguson, he doesn't look very good in pregame warm-ups. He just kind of looks like a guy." Well, he threw for 338 yards against us.

Florida State gnawed us up pretty good, gaining 569 yards and beating us 34-23. Ronnie Williams threw for 251 yards, Thurman ran for 97, and Hart Lee set a Gator Bowl record with eight catches for 104 yards, but we couldn't generate enough points to keep pace.

The season ended on a downer because we lost our last three games. But there was still big-time flavor to the whole thing, because it was the first time a group of OSU seniors was able to go to three consecutive bowls. Thurman Thomas, who began the year rampaging through Washington, was named a first-team All-American.

CHAPTER 10

Going with Gundy

1986

JACKPOT

Coaches will tell you recruiting is an inexact science, but we hit it big with two of our signees in 1986.

Barry Sanders was not highly recruited, but he became a Heisman Trophy winner and could have been the NFL's all-time leading rusher if things like that had been important to him.

Mike Gundy was a little undersized, but he was the state of Oklahoma's player of the year as a senior at Midwest City High School, and he finished his OSU career as the leading passer in Big Eight history.

Also in that 1986 recruiting class was Gerald Hudson, who became a starter after Sanders departed for the NFL and ended up leading the NCAA in rushing.

MAGIC MAN

When we were recruiting Gundy, we really couldn't make up our minds where he would fit into things. Louis Campbell was a pretty good judge of talent, and you could tell Mike had a little bit of magic about him, because he drove his high school team down the field 71 yards to beat Muskogee in the state championship game.

We finally said, "To heck with his height. Let's go get the guy because he's a winner." He had also visited Army, OU wanted him, and I think Arkansas tried to get in on him, too.

We thought we were going to get Mike, but when he visited OU, word got out the next day that he had committed there. We all panicked. I got him on the phone and asked him what was going on. Mike said something to the extent of, "Don't worry about it, Coach. They just got me in a room down there and I had to tell them I was coming or they weren't going to let me out."

The OU coaches had hot-boxed him—a recruiting thing. It wasn't bad. They just put the clamps on him pretty good, like it was an interrogation or something. Mike realized they were not going to let him out of there until he told them what they wanted to hear.

Later, Barry Switzer called Mike and Mike told Switzer he was going to Oklahoma State. I asked Mike what Switzer said, and Mike said Barry cussed him like a yard dog. Switzer didn't take it very well, but Gundy stuck with us.

Louis Campbell had a great relationship with Ray and Judy Gundy. I remember having a great visit down there. Cale, Mike's little brother who later played at OU, was also hanging around.

Mike made a legitimate decision for the right reasons and we got him even though we had a hard time getting kids from Midwest City. Most of those kids had always been OU people. We didn't know if some of them knew where Stillwater was, quite honestly. But Mike was a high-profile commitment for us. It was probably a little hard for him to pass on OU, but we had been to three straight bowls and were winning big. Mike had witnessed the big Bedlam shootouts, like the 1984 game and the Ice Bowl, so it wasn't just a left-field signing. We had credibility, and Mike knew that what we were doing offensively fit him better. OU wasn't going to scrap the wishbone for him. He had seen them go

with Jamelle Holieway—and rightfully so—over Troy Aikman. Mike probably could have run the wishbone. He was athletic enough to do it. But we told him the truth. He had a good relationship with our offensive coordinator, Larry Coker, and Louis Campbell had done a great job with him. So we got him.

GUT CHECK

What makes a coach decide a recruit is worth taking? I always relied on gut instinct.

There were a lot of intangibles that worked in Gundy's favor. He was a little bit older. He had a wrestling background, so we knew he was a tough guy. He stood his ground, for lack of a better term, against Switzer. And he had to show some spine to be a Midwest City kid and not go to OU.

Mike proved to be a real competitor. I think Brian Bosworth slung him down or something one time and Mike jumped right back up into his chest. In another instance, Mike goaded an Iowa State defensive lineman into getting ejected.

Of course, Mike became an assistant coach for us as soon as his playing career was over and now he is OSU's head coach. Back when he was a player, did I ever think the kid would someday be the Cowboys' head coach? There were signs early that he was special. I always tried to read kids' body language. He mixed right in with our veteran guys. We had high-profile, good players like Thurman Thomas, Hart Lee Dykes, and Mark Moore. He fit right in as one of the fellows. They respected him. They respected his toughness. That was the stuff I noticed.

The first time we put Mike in the huddle, bang, he had command of things. I thought he was always exceptional like that—in his body language and the way he handled himself.

Besides quarterbacking two 10-win teams, Mike Gundy was the leading passer in Big Eight history and ranks second in total offense.
Photo courtesy of Oklahoma State University

HIDDEN GEM

Barry Sanders, one of the best players in the history of the game, was pursued by three Division I schools: Oklahoma State, Tulsa, and Iowa State.

Let's state for the record that George Walstad was the hero concerning Sanders' recruitment. George was a veteran talent evaluator, had coached at Kansas State, and had coached high school ball in Wichita, Kansas, where Sanders played for North High School. George was our Kansas guy. He didn't need a road map up there, and he knew everybody.

I'm trying to remember the first time I ever heard George mention Sanders to me. Wichita North had a big lineman named Joel Fry, who was showing up on a lot of recruiting lists. We were in on Joel, and George said there was also a small back at Wichita North who had been bothered by a turned ankle and used as a wingback. That was Sanders. George talked like Sanders was a pretty interesting guy.

When we played up at Kansas during the 1985 season, we sent our coaches around to blanket the state. George told our guys where to check on kids. He took our running backs coach, Bill Shimek, and drove over to Wichita North.

While George was talking to the coaches, Bill watched some of their films. Bill didn't stay in there very long and when he came back, George made some remark to him like, "Are you through?"

Bill told him something along the lines of, "We don't need to watch any more of this film. We are crazy if we don't take this Sanders kid." So Bill confirmed what George already knew.

Keep in mind that we signed Gerald Hudson and two other highly regarded running backs that year. We beat OU and Stanford to sign Vernon Brown from Del City and everybody recruited Terrance Miller from Lewisville, Texas. Because of our success, we were dealing with a higher level of players across the board than in past years. But there was never a debate as to whether we were going to take Sanders.

We didn't necessarily put those backs in a pecking order, but Sanders wasn't spoken of in the same tones as Vernon Brown and Terrance Miller.

I know Barry visited Tulsa and Iowa State. The crazy part about it was that neither Kansas school showed interested in him. Maybe he got lost in the shuffle because Kansas and Kansas State were in transition periods with new coaches.

SECRET FILM

Bill Shimek apparently didn't want to take any chances that some other school might stumble onto Sanders.

I think when Shimek and Walstad were up at Sanders' high school, one game film featured Sanders as a wingback on a counter play. It opened your eyes a little bit.

Shimek brought the film back with him. They might have said they were bringing it back to show me and then just kept it or something.

People say Sanders was hidden, and it's true that he was, but Tulsa and Iowa State both did their work on him. There was nothing to stop OU from recruiting up there. But the crazy part of it was that in-state schools should have shown up on him, especially since people were already at the school for Joel Fry. He was pretty highly recruited. We got them both. Joel was given way more attention. But if people were going there to recruit Joel—which they were—they could have seen the same thing we saw. So Walstad was the hero.

I really don't remember if Sanders had any stats to speak of in high school, but we took him purely on skill level. Sanders began putting up stats pretty quickly. In a Kansas Shrine game before he reported to us, he ran for 211 yards and scored a couple of times. I remember George went up there to watch the game.

He came back and said, "This kid Sanders might be even better than we think he is, because he put on a show."

After Sanders got to campus, he put on another show for our strength coach, John Stuckey. Stuckey always ran a little battery of tests for our players—40s and cone drills and such. I want to say Gundy had a real good cone drill, but Sanders moved in a way we hadn't seen anybody move. You couldn't say at that time the guy was going to win a Heisman Trophy, but you immediately recognized he had some unique skills.

STICKS AND STONES

During the 1986 recruiting wars, we were in a race with OU and Iowa for Melvin Foster, a highly regarded prospect from Houston Yates.

Newspapers carried stories that accused Barry Switzer of telling Foster that one of our coaches, Willie Anderson, was going to be banned from coaching and that we were going to go on probation. The kid went to Iowa.

Negative recruiting, quite honestly, never really bothered me. There is a gray area as to what is and what isn't negative recruiting. I didn't put any stock into it one way or another. If somebody did so, that was his business.

Now, on the same hand, I didn't refute his accusation. I didn't refute it because I didn't have a good feeling. But I didn't think ill of Switzer. Negative recruiting is out there. It never really was a factor to me.

Willie resigned to enter private business in May of 1986 and we hired Johnny Barr to take his place. We also moved Kevin Steele from our offensive to defensive staff after Reggie Herring left to go to Auburn.

HOOP DREAMS

A basketball game may have cost Thurman Thomas a chance to win a Heisman Trophy.

In June of '86, Thurman injured his knee playing basketball. I think he just went up for a shot, wasn't even touched, and a ligament popped.

My future wife, Becky, and I were getting ready to take our annual summer trip to Maui, something we looked forward to every year. The night before we left, our trainer, Jeff Fair, called me and said, "You are not going to like this."

Jeff told me about Thurman. I told him to do whatever they had to do, because there was nothing I could do about it now. And I knew our orthopedic guy, Cary Couch, was a really talented doctor.

The funny thing about the whole deal is that they opened up Thurman and decided not to do anything. They might have cleaned his knee up some, but whatever ligament it was, Cary's opinion was that it was one he could do without. It sounds bad, but if your quads are strong enough, you can play—your knee might go out next season or it might never go out. In this case, it never did, four Super Bowls and a Pro Football Hall of Fame career later.

But Thurman's knee was a concern going into that season, and we were pretty guarded with him toward the end of two-a-days, which he didn't like.

Thurman had been a first-team All-American and was 10th in Heisman voting in 1985, but he had a down year—774 yards—after his knee injury in 1986, although he still made All-Big Eight.

If Thurman hadn't injured the knee, he might have had a good enough season in '86 to build momentum for a Heisman Trophy campaign as a senior in '87. He had two big years as a freshman and sophomore and could have been "the guy" going into his senior year. Instead, he was seventh in Heisman voting as a senior.

That basketball injury also explains why Thurman was not picked until the second round of the 1988 NFL Draft. Half the NFL teams wouldn't pass him on his physical exam because the ligament was not there. It cost him being a first-round pick, though he proved to everybody he should have been a first-round guy.

Even though I wish Thurman had not been hurt, I never implemented a basketball ban for my players. Now, if there had been a big tangle where a bunch of guys got into a fight playing basketball, I probably would have. But Sanders played over in the Colvin Center. They all played over there. We always told them to be careful and not to do anything stupid. Thurman literally just went up for a shot when the knee popped. It was a hard-luck year for Thurman. A bee even stung him inside his helmet when we played at Houston.

ALMOST AMBUSH

We opened the 1986 season at Southwestern Louisiana. This was a scary game because they made such a big promotion out of it. It was the first time they had played a Big Eight team. Nelson Stokley was coaching his first game down there and we had no idea what they were going to run. They ended up running the spread option, an option strain of the run-and-shoot.

Their quarterback was Brian Mitchell, who later played for a long time with the Washington Redskins, retiring as the NFL's all-time kick-return leader. No one could get him down in the NFL, so it's no wonder we couldn't pen him up. He must have run forever.

We looked like we were dead in the water when Southwestern Louisiana scored to go up 20-9 with 3:24 left. Bobby Riley gave us a chance when he returned the kickoff 97 yards for a touchdown and, after we got a stop, Ronnie Williams took us down the field and threw an 11-yard fade to Hart Lee Dykes with eight seconds left for a 21-20 win.

We should have lost the dadgum ballgame. That's why I don't blame big programs for their reluctance to play road games against such schools. They gave us quite a bit of money to go down there, but we were as lucky as the devil to get out of there with a win. I knew then that we still had quite a bit of work to do.

OMINOUS SIGNS

We had some rebuilding to do in the offensive line in 1986 and we were beaten up at running back that year, which helped Sanders move up the depth chart quickly.

After a 27-23 loss at Tulsa, there was reason to be concerned about our defense, which had given up 850 yards in two games, and our quarterback. Ronnie had thrown four interceptions, and two were returned for touchdowns. He also had another interception against Tulsa that they converted into a 19-yard touchdown drive. I told the media after the Tulsa game that Ronnie was the guy we needed to have in there and that I liked Ronnie, but I had seen all the turnovers I wanted to see.

MAKING A CHANGE

Ronnie was 11-of-21 with an interception when we played Houston in our third game. We trailed 21-3 at halftime.

I pulled the trigger on a quarterback change and, on the way to the locker room, I told our true freshman quarterback, Mike Gundy, "Go find the center and take some snaps, because you're going to play the second half."

Mike did a double take, but I said this was for real and he was the guy.

I had asked our offensive coaches a week before if we could get Gundy a few more reps in practice, because we felt good about him and I could see a change coming. I think we gave him some reps with the second team, not the first, since we knew this was going to be a delicate situation.

At the time, Rodderick Gaines was listed as No. 2 behind Ronnie, and Gundy was No. 3.

If we were to promote Gundy past Gaines, would we have problems with Gaines?

And, more importantly, Ronnie was a popular guy who was very close to Thurman, Hart, and Mark Moore. But I told Larry Coker this coaching decision was a case-closed deal and we weren't going to have any discussion about it. I told him I would break the news to Ronnie.

I told Larry to be as limited as he needed to be with Gundy in the second half and to call the stuff he knew. We trotted Mike out there and he hit 12-of-22 throws for 163 yards and a touchdown in the second half. We lost 28-12, but we saw enough of Mike to realize the guy had some spunk about him. This was a get-him-going game—we had to find out what he was all about.

DAMAGE CONTROL

I found Ronnie at halftime of the Houston game and told him we were going with Gundy. If I remember right, his helmet ricocheted across the shower room. I didn't expect anything less, because Ronnie was a competitive guy.

I had a pretty good heart-to-heart talk about the change with Thurman and Hart. They were two high-profile players as well as leaders on the team, and they had questioned it. I went over to their apartment and saw them because I was concerned about how they would take it.

I told them something to the effect that, ultimately, this thing was going to work out and just to trust me on it. They did, but they still had a lot of personal loyalty to Ronnie.

I made sure we didn't cast Ronnie aside. He was a good enough athlete that we moved him to receiver. I went to our receivers coach, Houston Nutt, and told him to get Ronnie in the rotation. Any other assistant coach could have been a knucklehead and said, "He's got to earn his way in," but Nutt and I were on the same page. We tried to make sure Ronnie was utilized.

Had Ronnie been the kind of guy to bow up in the aftermath of all this, it could have really wrecked our football team. If he had come in singing the blues and wanting to transfer, it wouldn't have been any fun. We had the possibility of racial issues, because he was black and Gundy was white. But I thought Ronnie's reaction was one of the most powerful events the whole time I was there. Ronnie handled it about as well as a man could handle it.

Keep in mind that this was a guy who was highly recruited and led us to the Gator Bowl and, with his jaw wired shut, threw for all those yards against Nebraska the year before. We loved the guy. But he was turnover-prone and we had Mike in the wings. We needed to get Mike going. We just had to do it.

Ronnie played in the NFL, had a good career, and made some money. I was reunited with him later on when we were both with the Dolphins. He's down in Wichita Falls now and doing well.

It obviously worked out. Dykes was afraid he might never catch a pass again, but he still became the all-time leading receiver in the history of the Big Eight. It played out better than any of us thought it would. But of all the guys that went through that program in the 16 years I was there, there was nobody I had more respect for than Ronnie Williams.

BORROWING FLUTIE'S PLAYBOOK

Boston College decided to start Doug Flutie when he was a freshman, just as we did with Gundy. I knew Boston College's coach, Jack Bicknell, reasonably well, and we spoke about how they used Flutie.

I thought Gundy had a little bit of Flutie in him. They were both smaller, runaround-type quarterbacks. It might have been

Jack who told me they did a scramble drill to take advantage of Flutie's mobility.

We beat Illinois State 23-7 in Gundy's first start, but the event was more notable because Barry Sanders got his first 100-yard game, carrying 25 times for 132 yards.

BIG RED DOUBLEHEADER

We had to play third-ranked Nebraska and fifth-ranked Oklahoma, both on the road, in our next two games.

We hung in pretty well against Nebraska for what we were at the time. We lost 30-10, holding them to 333 yards with an interception return by Jerry Deckard for a touchdown. We might have had a chance if Nebraska hadn't gotten loose for 214 return yards.

Oklahoma beat us 19-0 and I told the media after the game that I had never been prouder of any group of guys. The Sooners were leading the nation in rushing, but they didn't get an offensive touchdown against us. They scored on an interception return and kicked four field goals. OU was a 33-point favorite, but we battled them tooth and nail.

Even though we lost those two games and fell to 2-4, we gained confidence and momentum that helped us salvage a winning season.

BACK ON TRACK

We split games with Kansas and Colorado to fall to 3-5. Gundy didn't like losing and told reporters Colorado was never going to beat OSU again while he was there.

I met with seniors like Mark Moore to talk about what goals were still attainable. Those seniors had been to three straight bowls and it was a shame that things were not going right for them.

We got hot and swept our last three games against Kansas State, Iowa State, and Missouri. Gundy started to throw it around pretty good, and Hart's fear that he would never catch another ball quickly vanished. His 11 receptions against Iowa State were the most since Hermann Eben's 12 catches against OU in 1969.

We agreed to move a game against Missouri to December for ESPN, my biggest regret that season. They gave both Missouri and us some money to do it, but it probably cost us a bowl game.

We beat Missouri to finish 6-5. If we had played the game earlier in the year when it was originally scheduled, we would have been in position to lobby for a bowl. But when the bowl bids came out we were sitting at 5-5, and everybody had already cut their deals. No bowl could promise us anything because we didn't know if we were going to have a winning record.

Seven wins normally got a team into a bowl during that day. Even though we were 6-5, I still think we would have been attractive to bowl executives because we had been to three straight bowls and we had the box-office draw of Thurman and a hot young quarterback.

I'm confident we would have gone somewhere—the Independence Bowl or something similar. When we decided to move the Missouri game, we probably thought we would have more wins and the date of the game wouldn't be a factor. It was my fault for agreeing to move it.

PASSING GRADE

We had three 10-win seasons while I was at Oklahoma State, but I think winning four of our last five games and guiding this group to a 6-5 record might have been our best coaching job.

We had to rebuild the line. We went through a pretty traumatic quarterback change. We lost Bobby Riley, our second-leading receiver, to an injury. Thurman was up and down, even though he was All-Big Eight. Several of our other backs were hurt. We lost one of our offensive linemen, Mike Wolfe, to an injury at midseason. We put up with a lot more injury-wise than in other years.

I think playing well in those losses to Nebraska and OU helped this particular group of guys really start building, and that carried over into our last four wins—which in turn spilled over into 20 wins the next two years. Finishing strong really set the stage for fireworks in 1987 and 1988.

CHAPTER 11

Christmas in El Paso

1987

COULD'VE BEEN COWBOYS

Even though 1986 was a down year by our standards, we were still getting visits from high-level recruits because of our success in previous seasons. But when it got right down to it, the fact that we were under NCAA investigation scared kids, and rightfully so. I didn't blame them.

Who were some of the prospects who might have gone to Oklahoma State if not for the NCAA probe? How about Bam Morris, who had a great career at Texas Tech and played for the Pittsburgh Steelers in a Super Bowl; Greg Hill, a great back at Texas A&M and a first-round draft pick of the Kansas City Chiefs; and Will Shields, who won the Outland Trophy at Nebraska and might be in the Pro Football Hall of Fame someday?

Shields was a Lawton kid. I remember reading in the *Lincoln Journal Star* that Shields was quoted as saying he wanted to go to Oklahoma State, but the probation obviously derailed him and he went to Nebraska.

Greg Hill wanted to come. His mother would not let him. That's what he was telling us. He wanted to major in radio and

TV, and they had just built that new radio/TV facility here. He was enamored with it. But A&M did a good job with him and they got him.

The NCAA issues were brought up against us at virtually every stop. I couldn't, in good faith, sit in some kid's living room and say there was nothing going on with the NCAA. Now, some people at the university tried to use semantics. Have you gotten the official letter of investigation? No. Well, who are those guys down the hall with briefcases? I knew what was going on. I would do what I had to do to get a kid, but I wasn't going to sit there and lie to people in their homes if they asked me about it. I was up front with them.

FREE AGENTS

SMU was forced to temporarily drop football when the NCAA gave the school the "death penalty." Its players were granted the freedom to transfer anywhere and were immediately eligible.

We had already hired one of SMU's coaches, a former OU player named Kenith Pope. We didn't hire Kenny because we thought he could help us get some of his old players. We were going to hire him anyway. But it seems like one of Kenny's first assignments was to go back down there and see if he could bring any Mustangs to Stillwater.

We ended up with two SMU players, Kim Johnson and Kenneth Grant. Kim helped us instantly. He had one year of eligibility left, but was worth taking. He had been a center at SMU, but became a defensive lineman for us, playing both ways in at least one game.

We picked up another kid a year earlier when Drake dropped football. Our guys somehow knew Brien Keith, a tight end up there. We didn't need a starter because we had J.R. Dillard, but we more or less ended up with two starters because of Keith. He was a good player for us in 1986 and '87.

BIGGER THAN LIFE

Jaime Cardriche was another "free agent" that we put on scholarship, courtesy of OSU's basketball coach at the time, Leonard Hamilton.

Leonard told me he had a big kid who had played some football before. Jaime was a huge guy. He was 6-foot-9 and 345 pounds. But I knew that Leonard just wanted us to pick up Jaime's scholarship so it would free up a basketball scholarship for someone else. I said, "Let's just cut through all this other stuff, and if you need me to put him on aid, I will."

Jaime never got on the field during a game, but he was actually pretty gifted. I could see he had pretty good hand-eye coordination for a big guy, but he couldn't hold up to the heat. The whole pace of things was way, way too much for him and I think he finally just quit.

It turned out Jaime had talents beyond football and basketball. He became a pro wrestler and actor. He was in several TV shows and movies before dying in July of 2000 at age 32. He was perhaps best known for playing Tim in the TV series *Malcolm and Eddie*.

VENGEANCE IS THURMAN'S

Thurman Thomas went about spring drills with a vengeance because he wanted to prove how good he was.

We had been guarded with him in spring practice the year before and, although he was named All-Big Eight after the knee injury, he had what he considered a sub-par year. This was the start of his senior year and we couldn't get him out of the huddle in the tough drills, the inside run drills, or the scrimmages.

If we ever tried to take him out, he wouldn't go. He wanted to prove to himself and everybody else that he was back, like, "If anybody thinks I am damaged goods, they are kidding themselves." And he set the tone anyway.

We wanted to get Barry Sanders reps with the first unit—and we did—but on the same hand, Thurman wouldn't take a break. I don't think Thurman was motivated by the continuing emergence of Sanders, because he was confident enough in his own ability. But I think he practiced with a chip on his shoulder, which tended to make everyone else tougher. All those other guys were better off because of Thurman.

LOADED BACKFIELD

We had two future Pro Football Hall of Famers on our tailback depth chart. Those guys were so talented that people probably don't realize how good the backs behind them were. We could have lined up Vernon Brown and Mitch Nash and done really well.

There's an interesting recruiting story in regard to Nash, a former Oklahoma high school player of the year.

Larry Coker and I went to Bartlesville to have dinner with Mitch and his family. They were really nice people, but we lost our appetite pretty quickly when they announced to us before dinner that Mitch had decided to go to Oklahoma.

We learned a lesson from Mitch's recruitment. We didn't try to talk him out of going to OU. We just told him to make sure he was doing it for the right reasons. Our advice was, "Sleep on it, and if you wake up in the morning and you feel totally right about it, then you've done the right thing. We wish you well and we think a lot of you, regardless of where you choose to go to school."

The next morning, Mitch had his high school coach, Mickey Ripley, contact us. Mitch said he had changed his mind. So Mickey contacted Larry, who went back up to Bartlesville. The kid said, "What you guys said last night hit home and I woke up this morning and didn't feel right. I want to go to OSU."

Mickey Ripley was a former OU player. Mickey didn't have to call Larry. He just as easily could have called Merv Johnson over at OU and said, "Merv, you need to get over here and straighten this kid out." But Mickey did what the kid wanted him to do.

If we had bowed up in Mitch's home trying to hammer OU, I don't think the kid would have ever changed his mind. Instead, we stepped aside gracefully, no hard feelings, and didn't burn bridges. Taking the high road paid off.

There are some kids that you can take the opposite approach with, but Mitch was a good kid, and his reasons for wanting to go to OU were valid.

Mitch was a very good back for us, and when he played, he played well. He was a valued player, a great individual, and never a problem. As a highly decorated guy, Mitch had chances to go elsewhere, but we got him and he was a heck of a teammate all the way through.

SHOOTOUT AT O-STATE CORRAL

Traditionally, I spoke to our regents before the first home game. I looked like a prophet in 1987 when I told them they might want to watch our return game. Sanders returned the opening kickoff 100 yards for a touchdown—the first shot fired in one of the all-time shootouts.

We beat Tulsa 39-28. I remember that Bill Connors, the *Tulsa World's* sports editor, called it a wildly entertaining game. We combined for nearly 1,000 yards of offense and they started a freshman quarterback, T.J. Rubley, who threw for 386 yards in his first start.

We finally broke the game open late, but we could never really stop them.

Thurman Thomas ran for 164 yards and we won, perhaps because we had the finest collection of offensive skill players in school history. On the other hand, I could tell that our defensive talent level was slipping. We weren't very good and were really scrambling in our front seven, but we did have enough speed to create turnovers.

Melvin Gilliam was our only returning starter in the secondary. We rebuilt the defensive backfield around him and he was the ringleader of that group.

Melvin had been a *Parade* All-American in high school and was athletic enough to play for the Oklahoma State basketball team. We used to joke that Melvin thought he could play quarterback, but he really was a good football player. He was smart and he was tough and his instincts were great. He had a fantastic feel for the game.

RUN AND SHOOT BLANKS

Tulsa gained the most yards against an Oklahoma State team since Nebraska in 1979. Next we had to face a run-and-shoot Houston team coached by Jack Pardee.

I remember telling our defensive staff that I thought we were going to match up pretty well with them. I said I would be surprised if we didn't shut them out. They thought I had lost my mind, because Jack Pardee had just come out of the USFL, and his teams with Jim Kelly put up all kinds of big numbers.

But we went down there and beat them like a drum, giving up only 266 yards in a 35-0 rout. They got a pretty rude awakening, but Pardee was laying the foundation for that group of kids, who set records with Andre Ware at quarterback. I remember them putting Ware in late in the game, but Sanders took a punt back for a score and Thurman ran for 111 yards.

WELCOME, SOONERS

We got a surprise when we pulled in at the team hotel for our game at Wyoming the next week. Right there on the marquee of the Holiday Inn in Laramie were the words "Welcome, University of Oklahoma."

Our athletic director, Myron Roderick, saw that, got all mad, and went in to crawl all over the hotel people. I suspect that Wyoming's coach, Paul Roach, had something to do with it. I knew Paul reasonably well. I asked him if that hotel marquee was intentionally incorrect and he just smiled.

Wyoming was a good offensive football team and we never trailed, but we had to hold on to win 35-29 in a game that featured 1,156 offensive yards. Our strong safety, Rod Smith, recovered two fumbles and intercepted a pass. His takeaways led to 17 points.

We had trouble getting the ball away from them, but they couldn't handle us, either. Thurman ran for 193 yards, Gundy threw for 325, and Dykes caught eight balls for 154 yards. Sanders had a run in which he ran into the pile, reversed his field, and sprinted a long way.

EXTRA POINTS

If I remember correctly, Wyoming scored right at the end of the game. At that time, if both coaches agreed, you didn't even have to attempt an extra point if you scored on the final play of regulation.

Well, for some reason Paul Roach decided to go for two, even though it was irrelevant and the game was over. Their quarterback got busted up on the conversion attempt. They carted the kid off and I think he was OK, but he looked like he was really hurting. I remember asking Paul later why he chose to run a play. He had forgotten about the rule or something like that.

I gave Ronnie Williams the game ball afterward. Ronnie, both a good leader and a good guy, is the kid we moved from quarterback to receiver. We respected him as much as anybody in the 16 years I was there, bar none. It was among the first game balls I had given to a player. The previous season I gave one to a lineman, Mike Zentic, who played a game immediately after having his knee scoped.

MAKING HISTORY

Despite our defensive liabilities, we beat Southwestern Louisiana 36-0, shutting out our second opponent in four games. Our players viewed it as a revenge game. Even though we had beaten them the year before, we had to come from behind to win it at the end.

Sweeping the first four games put us in position for a record of 5-0 for the first time since 1945. Getting to 5-0 was a difficult chore in previous seasons, because we opened league play against Nebraska every year from 1983 to 1986.

In 1987, we were going to open league play against Colorado, who had beaten us the year before and gone to a bowl. This was a big game for a lot of reasons, but we tore them up pretty good, winning 42-17. I know it stunned Colorado. They didn't expect it. They thought it was going to be a close ballgame.

We forced six turnovers to break the game open. At the time, we led the nation in turnover margin.

AT THE MOVIES

We were No. 12 in the AP poll when second-ranked Nebraska came to Stillwater for a nationally televised game in 1987. The outcome—Nebraska won 35-0—wasn't particularly memorable, but I will always remember what happened the night before the game.

We took our guys to the movie theater and, coincidentally, Nebraska was there too.

When we went to a movie, I had rules. I wouldn't let players roam around the theater, so we had regulations as to when they could buy popcorn and everything. We didn't want anything goofy to happen.

Well, the Nebraska coaches let their players wander around, go in and out, and hang around the lobby. As we were leaving, some sort of exchange occurred between their players and our players. We were almost on the bus when I heard Thurman, Hart, and some others cussing behind me.

Their coaches and our coaches realized that we needed to get this under control pretty quickly. When we finally got our guys on the bus, Nebraska's Broderick Thomas approached. Broderick was a great player and good guy who liked to talk a lot. All of a sudden, it got started again—hollering and finger-pointing from the bus. I think it was Dykes who yelled something very politically incorrect about Broderick's mental capacity.

No punches were thrown as far as I know, but there were a lot of verbal spars and hand gestures that night.

They got on us pretty good the next day, and the fact that we didn't play them any better at home was our biggest disappointment that season. But, with such great players as Neil Smith, they were the best Nebraska defense I had seen.

Before the '87 season, Broderick did an interview in which he brought up some allegations regarding the NCAA and us. He later denied it and, a few days later, was jailed for resisting arrest.

I coached in the NFL after leaving Oklahoma State. A few years ago, before a preseason game with the 49ers, I was sitting outside the stadium. I looked around and there was a guy in 49er coaching gear. I didn't recognize him at first, but he said, "Hey Coach, it's the Sandman," which was Broderick's nickname.

We sat there for a long time and had a great visit. Broderick, Hart Lee, and all those Houston-area guys tended to tease each other a great deal. But to this day, I like Broderick. We never had a problem.

FIGHTING CHANCE

Maybe we didn't get all the scrapping out of our system during the movie theater incident, because we almost got into a brawl the next week at Missouri.

One of our offensive linemen, Doug Meacham, was the first guy to blow by me after them. Doug is an assistant coach at OSU now. I don't remember what started the fight, but we had a pretty good tangle. Guys didn't get thrown out, but benches were emptied.

Missouri was ranked sixth nationally in rushing that season, but we beat them 24-20 when Mike Gundy threw a touchdown pass to J.R. Dillard with 7:46 left. We trailed 17-7 at halftime and gambled on a fourth-down play to set up the winning touchdown. Rather than attempt a field goal into the wind on a fourth-and-nine play, Gundy threw an 18-yard pass to Dykes, who caught the ball even though the guy defending him was flagged for pass interference.

PICK YOUR POISON

Thurman and Barry both rushed for more than 100 yards in a 56-7 Halloween homecoming slaughter of Kansas State. We led 28-0 in the first quarter, and the score could have been as lopsided as we wanted it to be.

Juggling carries for Thomas and Sanders was never a problem because of the way they felt about each other. We started some sort of rotation for them early that season. Thurman would play the first three series, Barry the next three, and then they would alternate themselves.

We asked Sanders to defer to Thurman since he had seniority, but I can't remember it ever being an issue. I can remember Thurman making a long run and taking himself out on the goal line so Sanders could go in. It was a great arrangement.

The next week against Oklahoma, we actually started Thurman and Barry in the same backfield in a power-I formation. I wanted to get them both out there and do a little something different, even though we were essentially running the same plays. But we had a good receiver corps, so we didn't want to just load up the backfield and use a one-receiver formation. I think it was the only time we started Sanders and Thurman together, although we occasionally put them in the game at the same time.

THIS BOTHERED ME

We were 28 ½-point underdogs against Oklahoma and lost 29-10. That game really bothered me and it stayed with me for a while. We had a chance to win it, and the final score was very deceptive.

We had a possession to win the game in the fourth quarter. We thought they had knocked J.R. Dillard down on a crossing route when Troy Johnson intercepted a pass and ran it back for a touchdown.

We drove back down the field, still hoping we could score and get an onside kick. Then Rickey Dixon intercepted a pass and returned it for a touchdown with 32 seconds left.

We had done everything we needed to do to win—Thurman even accumulated 173 yards—and we had a very legitimate chance. Those interception returns distorted the game. We played our butts off against the nation's fifth-ranked team. I told the media after the game that we had a good football team and they were silly if they wrote anything different. But that game bothered me maybe as much as any game during my time there. I shouldn't have let it, but I did.

PAT TO THE RESCUE

This was the Bedlam game in which OU's quarterback, Jamelle Holieway, wrecked his knee right in front of me. I immediately ran out on the field and told him to lie down slowly and stay calm. I also hollered for their trainer, Dan Pickett, who was already on his way.

Why did I do it? I know there is a lot of alleged bad blood in Bedlam and all that. But here was a fellow competitor and great player right in front of me. I saw him hop, and when he started crumpling up, I went out and grabbed him. I just didn't want him to fall. Everything became irrelevant. A competitive kid fell down in front of me and I went out there and got him. All of the Bedlam stuff became meaningless.

To this day, I still get letters from OU people concerning that act. Now that I am doing a sports radio show, I get a couple of calls per year about it.

FINISHING KICK

We beat the brains out of Kansas the next week and the score, 49-17, didn't do justice to how lopsided the matchup was.

A funny thing happened at the end of the game. They scored a meaningless touchdown, so somebody yelled, "Get the kickoff return team out there!" Sanders ran past me before I could grab him. He was an All-America kick returner that season, but I didn't want him out there because it wasn't worth risking an injury.

George Walstad, our special teams coach, told me to stay calm because Kansas wouldn't kick it to Sanders anyway. Their kicker tried to squib it and hit a line shot. It took one hop, and Sanders ran it back 99 yards for a score.

I apologized to KU's coach, Bob Valesente, after the game and he said not to worry about it; it was their fault for kicking to him.

PECKING ORDER

Thurman and Barry combined for 318 rushing yards against Kansas. Thurman ran for 202 yards, becoming OSU's all-time total offense leader. Thurman could have been a Heisman frontrunner that season if he hadn't injured his knee the year before. Sanders would win the Heisman in '88.

Anyhow, I had two Pro Football Hall of Fame running backs on my team at the same time. People have asked me to choose who was better. Let me answer the question this way: Sanders is Michael Jordan. Thurman is Larry Bird. Larry Bird was a great player. Thurman was a great player.

Thurman led Buffalo to four straight Super Bowls. Sanders was unique and could make the world's greatest four-yard runs. But of all the guys I have ever coached to this day, I think if I had to spend the night with a guy in a foxhole, I would pick Thurman Thomas. He's tough. He's loyal. He's a great worker. He's smart. He's competitive. He's got a ton of energy about him. He's got a smile on his face all the time. Every day is a good day. He is just an unbelievable guy to be around.

I always used the word "warrior" in regard to Thurman. Sanders was more rapid. There is nobody like him. But Thurman is the toughest guy I have been around, bar none.

TOO MUCH THURMAN

Thurman became OSU's career rushing leader in his final regular-season game when he ran for the most yards ever, 293, against Iowa State. Their coach, Jim Walden, got a little bit mad at us and said something along the lines of, "I hope they got Thurman Thomas enough yards today" in his postgame press conference.

We knew Thurman was close to a record and we were going to get it for him. He deserved it. He was a first-team All-American, and he edged Nebraska quarterback Steve Taylor for Big Eight offensive player of the year honors that season.

In hindsight, Walden's comments are sort of amusing. Had we put Thurman on the bench, Barry Sanders would have been

Thurman Thomas was a cornerstone of four Super Bowl teams with the Buffalo Bills and was inducted in the Pro Football Hall of Fame in 2007.
Photo courtesy of Oklahoma State University

running against them. If we had him in there, he would have been breaking off long runs too.

We won 48-27, but I never really felt secure. We led only 33-27 until Thurman scored two touchdowns in the last five minutes. A lot of people had big days for us. Mike Gundy set single-season records for passing yards and touchdowns. Hart Lee Dykes became OSU's career leader in receiving yards. And we set a school single-season scoring record that would be broken again the following year.

PLAYING TROJANS?

We agreed to go to the Sun Bowl in El Paso to play USC, unless USC happened to upset UCLA in the last game of the regular season. We had options, but we really liked the lure of playing a tradition-rich program like USC.

Well, USC beat UCLA and we got matched against a 6-5 West Virginia team. This presented a whole different problem that I will talk about later. But I'll drop this hint: Thank goodness for rapping.

BOOT CAMP

The Sun Bowl people did a great job making sure we had a good time. They always assigned a guy to take the head coach around, and one day he and I made a stop in an industrial area. He took me into a place with a whole bunch of cowboy boots lining the wall. It was a custom boot manufacturer. Classically, they always built the respective Sun Bowl coaches a pair of boots.

I didn't really wear or know anything about boots, but they let me pick out the style, toe, heel, and everything else. All kinds of people were there making boots with leather and all these exotic materials. They told me to pick out whatever I wanted. I saw some beautiful tan-looking stuff—a kind of lizard skin or reptile or something. They didn't have enough of it to make the whole boot, but they used it to make the toe and the heel. They measured my foot and told me they would put the OSU brand, my initials, and the whole shebang on them. I asked how much the boots would cost if they weren't complimentary and I was told about $3,000.

I went back to practice bragging to our assistant coaches about the $3,000 boots I was getting for free. A lot of these guys were boot guys, so they were all impressed.

Bill Shimek had been out to the Sun Bowl several years before when he was at OU. Bill said to me, "I don't know if you know this or not, but they let Barry Switzer do the same thing.

They took Switzer out there and let him pick out a pair of boots, but two months later he got the boots with a bill in the box."

I was worried. I didn't even wear boots and I was fixing to get a $3,000 bill for one pair. But Bill was just having fun with me. He lied about it. I went through the whole practice thinking that they were going to send me a bill for those boots.

BORDER PATROL

Juarez is right across the border from El Paso, but I had put Mexico off-limits to our players unless it was an official part of the Sun Bowl activities.

That didn't last. I later found out they were going over there anyway.

But the Sun Bowl workers took us to a bullfight in Mexico. We had dinner and a bunch of margaritas. Later in the evening, they brought out a little baby bull and asked for volunteer bullfighters from the audience.

George Walstad, one of our coaches, had been into the margaritas pretty good. I looked over and saw George going down to the bullring. George went out, ole'd the bull several times, and the players all cheered.

I eventually got into the ring too, but for a different reason. Either George or one of the Sun Bowl executives had lost their car keys, so the three of us were crawling around on our hands and knees in the ring trying to locate those keys after everybody left.

RAPPER'S DELIGHT

I was worried our players weren't excited to play against a 6-5 West Virginia team. But the Mountaineers had lost four games by five or fewer points and they had good players, including quarterback Major Harris, who led them to an unbeaten regular season the next year.

After the Sun Bowl threw a barbecue for both teams, I didn't have to worry that we'd lack incentive anymore.

Both teams were supposed to do skits at the barbecue. That was when rapping was just getting started.

I knew what rapping was, but I hadn't heard much of it nor paid much attention to it. Well, Major Harris started rapping at this barbecue, beginning a back-and-forth deal. We had some rappers, too. Ruben Oliver, a good kid and nose guard from New Orleans, started rapping back at Major. Then it was on the verge of moving past rapping.

I caught the eye of West Virginia's coach, Don Nehlen. I gave Don the high sign. We knew we had better get those kids out of there. We blew a whistle and prematurely said, "The bus is going, so cut this thing off."

I tell you what that did for us. It snapped our guys out of it. We were practicing well anyway, but until that barbecue, we were worried that our guys weren't going to take them seriously.

WATCH NO. 21

CBS was doing the bowl game, so I met with their crew, Pat Haden, Brent Musburger, and John Dockery, the day before the game. Musburger asked me if there was anybody besides Thurman and Dykes and Gundy that he should know about.

I told him we had this other little back, sophomore Barry Sanders, who had made about half the All-America teams as a kick returner and could break this thing open.

Brent wrote it all down and, after observing Sanders' career, he still reminds me about that conversation.

LET IT SNOW

The Sun Bowl was on Christmas Day and we had a white Christmas. The second half was played in a pretty good snowstorm.

Thurman ran wild and we got out of our tailback rotation. Barry was OK with that because Thurman went after them with a passion, finishing with 157 yards and the MVP trophy.

We trailed 24-14 at halftime, but went ahead for good when Gundy threw a six-yard touchdown pass to J.R. Dillard late in the third quarter.

Sim Drain got a stop on a fourth-and-one play at our 26 with 10:37 left, and we later drove for a touchdown that Gundy kept alive with a 15-yard pass to Jarrod Green on third-and-eight.

We needed that extra touchdown. West Virginia drove down and cut the score to 35-33. Shawn Mackey, a freshman defensive lineman, saved the game for us when he tackled one of their players short of the goal line on a two-point conversion attempt with 1:13 left. Hart Lee Dykes recovered an onside kick and we wrapped up our second 10-win season in four years.

It was a good win and a good experience, because we had a great time out there.

We ended the season ranked No. 11. Had we beaten USC instead of West Virginia in the bowl game, it may have helped vault us into the top 10 of the final rankings.

CHAPTER 12

Run to the Heisman

1988

STRIKE A POSE

The 1988 season was a milestone in Oklahoma State's football history because Barry Sanders had the best year any running back had ever had—the NCAA used a lot of ink rewriting its record book—and he became the first and only Cowboy ever to win the Heisman Trophy.

Nowadays, guys get a lot of Heisman build-up before the season begins. Their schools buy billboard space or create Web sites or DVDs to promote candidates.

Barry Sanders won the Heisman by letting his actions speak for him, although our sports information director, Steve Buzzard, began sending out promotional information to the media once it became apparent Barry was a legit player in the Heisman race.

Keep in mind that Barry, at least in terms of national radar, was still a relative unknown prior to the 1988 season. Technically, he wasn't even a returning starter.

In fact, the question we got a lot before the '88 season was, "How in the world are you going to replace Thurman Thomas, who ran for more yards than anybody in OSU history?" We never did really hype people up in the preseason, so we kept it low key and said, "We've got a young man who was an All-America kick returner and we think we will be OK at tailback." We left it at that.

Sanders had split carries with Thurman in '87. Our coaches were curious to see what Barry could do with more playing time. We got our answer when he ran for 2,628 yards and scored 39 touchdowns—never mind that he spent about a third of the 1988 season on the bench while we blew people out.

FIGHTING HIS DEMONS

After hitting it big in the NFL, Dexter Manley came back for a former players function in the spring of 1988 and I let him address the team.

Dexter had been battling some personal demons. He expressed concern about coming back to Stillwater because he knew those former players would get together and some adult beverages would probably be consumed. Before he came, he called apologetically and asked if I knew anybody with Alcoholics Anonymous. I hooked him up with a friend of mine from AA and Dexter got a bit of moral support.

I felt a little sorry for Dexter, but we let him give a do-right talk to the team. Our players knew who he was and they had to be impressed by him because he was pretty physically imposing.

Dexter had done quite a bit of speaking and, for all that had surfaced about his illiteracy, his communication skills were pretty good when he wanted them to be. He gave the players a heck of a talk and got their attention in a couple of different ways. Shortly thereafter, Dexter went back to Washington D.C. He had some recurring issues with his demons, but hopefully his talk to our kids hit home.

People ask me about Dexter's claim that he could not read and I tell them I never did put a great deal of credibility in it. He wasn't a good student and I knew he struggled in the classroom, but I was his position coach and we were able to teach him football. So he was learning. I always prided myself in being able to teach guys who were not great learners. To me, the concerns over Dexter's illiteracy made things sound way worse than they were, and Oklahoma State publicly took some hits. Dexter wasn't that bad off and he is pretty shrewd in his maneuverings with the media. Faculty-wise, some people did look after him and probably did a few special favors for him, but on the same hand, he was better off when he left OSU than he was when he got there.

UNBALANCED TEAM

We had one of the best offenses in the history of college football in 1988. We led the nation in scoring (47.5 points per game) and ranked second to Utah in total yards.

If we had been as good defensively in '88 as we had been even after we came off probation with Jason Gildon, Keith Burns, and those guys, we might have won the national championship—or at least had a legitimate shot at it.

Our talent level on defense had started to erode before this season and we knew it. But we still had guys like Melvin Gilliam, Rod Smith, and Sim Drain, who could run around, hit people, and make plays.

I never felt comfortable with our defensive talent during this time. The rumors of probation and possible NCAA penalties were affecting our recruiting classes, although we still managed to bring in guys like Stacey Satterwhite and Mike Clark. But our front seven was not remotely the same as it had been in the past.

We battled on defense, so I can't fault us for that, but I was a little bit irritated at myself. We had gotten away from some Xs and Os I believed in and had gone in other directions. It was not the primary reason we struggled defensively—what we were doing was not at all unsound—but I regret that we got away from what we had done previously.

HOW GOOD ARE COWBOYS?

We were still an under-the-radar team entering the 1988 season even though we had won 10 games the year before. The AP only ranked 20 teams back then. We got enough preseason votes that we would have been 24th if the poll had been extended.

Miami, Ohio, found out how good we were in the opener. We beat them 52-20 and Sanders launched the season by returning the opening kickoff for a touchdown for an NCAA-record second consecutive season. Sanders ran for 178 yards, and Mike Gundy became OSU's all-time passing leader, even though he was only in the first game of his junior season.

ORANGE CRUSH

Our second game was a huge one. We were scheduled to play Texas A&M in Stillwater. The Aggies were a top-10 team the year before, when they roasted Notre Dame in the Cotton Bowl.

Texas A&M was coached by my old boss at Pitt, Jackie Sherrill. We had beaten them in 1983 in what was supposed to be the first game of a four-game series. Well, Jackie knew we were pretty good and that there was no penalty clause on our contractual agreement, so he just said they weren't going to play us and cancelled the other two games in the series.

We targeted this game because we knew we were good and, thanks to Mother Nature, it was a complete emotional trap for Texas A&M.

The week before they were supposed to play us, the Aggies were scheduled to play a home game against Alabama. It was a game A&M had circled on its calendar, especially since Jackie was an Alabama grad.

Well, Hurricane Gilbert was expected to come roaring into College Station that weekend. Alabama's coach, Bill Curry, did not want to put his team on a plane and fly through a hurricane, so on the Friday before the game he said that they weren't

Mike Gundy of Midwest City, Oklahoma, would later become an assistant coach and head coach at Oklahoma State.
Photo courtesy of Oklahoma State University

coming. I don't blame him. I wouldn't want to fly my team through a hurricane, either.

The game was not played that weekend, even though the weather was as clear as a bell in College Station. That was a big downer for the A&M people.

On the other hand, we were primed and ready to play them for a lot of reasons. This could be our statement game. It also became a fashion statement game when we broke out all-orange uniforms.

I can't remember if the kids asked me to do it or if it was my idea, but it was the first time we had worn orange pants and orange jerseys simultaneously. Night games in Stillwater have a pretty electric atmosphere anyway, but the crowd went bonkers when we came down that ramp wearing all orange.

Sanders ran 58 yards for a touchdown on the third play of the game, and the rout was on. We got up on them 17-0 and they had only run something like three plays. Bobby Raynor recovered a fumble on their first kickoff return, and Brandon Colbert recovered another one of their early fumbles. We scored the first six times we had the ball and beat them 52-15, which was as bad as we beat Miami, Ohio. A&M had good players, and Darren Lewis ran for 171 yards, but they were never in the game once the score snowballed on them.

MY BODYGUARD

We probably could have finished with 75 points on Texas A&M if we had wanted to run up the score. Sanders rushed for 157 yards. He was only in the game long enough to run for seven yards in the second half, though he did take a punt back for a score at the end of the third quarter.

Jackie Sherrill and I had a good relationship. He hired me at Pitt in 1978. But Jackie could be a little tempestuous, and an urban legend once spread that Jackie had gotten into a fight with one of the Pitt coaches.

Jackie was a competitive, prideful guy, and you never know what to say to somebody after beating him that badly, especially if it is somebody you know and respect. I have never felt comfortable with such situations. Knowing Jackie, I was a little fearful he would be aggravated. Our security guy usually stuck close after games, but I made sure to ask him to stay with me since Jackie might be mad.

Well, Jackie and I shook hands and I said, "Good luck" or something and went inside. But it wasn't over yet. After I went in the dressing room and talked to the media and a few recruits, somebody came by and told me Jackie was waiting for me in the lobby of the weight room and dressing room area. Uh oh. Again, I asked our security guy if he could kind of lurk around.

It really wasn't a surprise when Jackie came over, wished me luck, and complimented our football team. He was incredibly gracious.

I never really thought Jackie was going to explode on me. We had some minor recruiting tussles with A&M and I felt awkward about beating them so badly, but Jackie did not think we had tried to run up the score on them, and we hadn't. Jackie was a total gentleman and showed a lot of class, which didn't surprise me.

WAR PIGS

We knew we could score so rapidly that people were going to have to play uphill against us. College kids on other teams couldn't handle us offensively because they couldn't tackle Sanders or defend Dykes. Plus Gundy was hot, had some escape ability, and had other good receivers to throw to besides Dykes. We scored 41 or more points in all but one game that season.

I said earlier in this book that Nebraska's 1983 offense was the best in college football history. Skill position-wise, we were comparable or better. The difference was the caliber of players the Cornhuskers had on their offensive line, including Dean Steinkuhler, who won the Outland Trophy in '83.

But I would be doing a disservice to a great group of guys if I did not brag on the War Pigs. That was the nickname given to our starting offensive line of Mike Wolfe, Chris Stanley, John Boisvert, Jason Kidder, and Byron Woodard.

The War Pigs were veteran tough guys incredibly well coached by Brad Seely. We couldn't necessarily just line up and bulldoze good opponents, but we were going to get a hat on a hat and weren't going to bust a bunch of assignments. None of those guys got drafted, but I think they all went to NFL camps.

Of course, Barry Sanders was the kind of guy who couldn't care less about statistics and awards, but the War Pigs took a lot of pride in his accomplishments. They paid way, way more attention to his stats than he did.

HEISMAN MOMENTUM

We had done enough to be ranked No. 13 before playing Tulsa when Sanders started to accumulate respect, too. He ran for a school-record 304 yards and scored five touchdowns in a 56-35 win over the Golden Hurricane.

Tulsa coach David Rader compared Sanders to Bo Jackson, a Heisman winner from Auburn. Rader had coached at Alabama and seen Jackson first-hand. Jackson was more of a straight-line power runner and might have been faster, but nobody could jump sideways like Sanders.

Sanders' name started popping up in Heisman polls. We decided to throw on a little fuel because we knew what we had, but we didn't want to go completely goo-goo in terms of over-promotion. Steve Buzzard sent the media some mail-outs—a jazzed-up profile page—to let them know Sanders' accomplishments.

CALLING OFF THE DOGS

We were so productive offensively and Sanders was such a home-run hitter that he took an early seat on the bench in many games. In a 41-21 win over Colorado, which got us enough votes to rank 21st in the AP poll, Sanders got to carry the ball only four times after halftime. He gained 79 yards on his four second-half attempts.

A fan up in Boulder used to get on me something terrible. I tried not to pay attention to anybody in the stands. My dad warned me not to have rabbit ears. But this guy was close to the bench, screaming and cussing at me because he thought we were running up the score. We had the security guard join us because it looked like the screamer might jump down on the field and come after me.

I never said anything to the guy, but I remember staring at him once the game was out of hand. I just pointed to Sanders on the bench. I was trying to let the guy know that if I really wanted to run up the score, Sanders would have been in the game instead of sitting there with his helmet off.

A couple years later when we weren't very good, we went back to Boulder as Colorado was building a national championship team. I heard a female yelling at me in the stands. A student manager told me she was pretty attractive, so I turned around to look. The gal was seated next to the guy who screamed at me in 1988. He had come back to haunt me. He said, "I got you," after his lady friend made me look. We both laughed about it.

PICTURE PERFECT

Sports Illustrated did a piece on us when we were at Colorado. They had a great picture of Dykes catching the ball in full stride. At that time, he wore towels on the back of his pants so he could wipe off his hands. He would write little sayings on the towels. The NCAA later made kids stop doing it, but on that full-page picture of Dykes, you could see the towel. I think it said either "bye bye" or "see you."

The other picture was of Sanders jumping over the goal line. He was the master of jumping over everybody on goal-line plays. In the picture they took, he was parallel to the ground and as high as the heads of those Colorado defenders. It was just a stunning shot.

HUSKER HARVEST

I knew before we played Nebraska that we were very good offensively, but I began to realize we might have one of the all-time greatest offensive units after we scored 42 on them in Lincoln—the most points ever scored against a Tom Osborne-coached team and the most points anybody had scored against the Cornhuskers on their turf since 1949.

In most years, 42 points would be enough to beat Nebraska. We gave up 63 points.

On their first play, the Cornhuskers pitched it to Ken Clark, who went 73 yards for a touchdown. From our sideline, it looked like the New York Life commercial. I was watching our guys run to the ball when all of a sudden everybody just got cut. Nobody was standing up. They all got their legs cut out from under them. He ran and scored.

We wanted to go down there and counter, but they got an interception and ran it back 86 yards for a score. The thing continued to snowball and, by the time we ran 12 plays, they led 35-0. It was still the first quarter.

We had a good football team, but I was doing addition in my head, figuring they might score 100 on us. When you are in Lincoln and things start going south on you, it's probably one of the hardest places in all of football, pro or college, to try to get straightened out.

The frustrating thing is we were both ranked in the top 10 and we had a legitimate chance to win if we could have just stopped them a few times. We scored 21 points in the second quarter, but had too much ground to make up. They were so far ahead that we couldn't catch them, but they couldn't stop us and had to leave their starters in the game. It wasn't like we were getting our points against down-the-line guys.

We just were bamboozled at the start. It was really a weird, weird game. Our lack of defense was even more glaring against quality opponents, but we didn't have any more moves to make on that side of the ball.

BEDLAM TUNE-UPS

Our game against Oklahoma in 1988 would prove to be one of the most memorable—and controversial—in series history.

Before we played Oklahoma, we had to play a Missouri team that stacked its defense to stop Sanders and a bad Kansas State team that put up a pretty good fight against us.

Sanders got 133 yards against Missouri and didn't play in the last 11 minutes. It was a pick-your-poison deal for the Tigers, who let Dykes catch five balls for 135 yards.

Kansas State was desperate enough to try consecutive onside kicks against us, and they recovered both, which agitated us. Sanders ran 37 times for 320 yards, becoming the first back in NCAA history to have two 300-yard games in a season. Afterward, Kansas State coach Stan Parrish asked me to go into their dressing room to talk to their kids. I said I respected them as competitors and told them to stay the course. We "only" beat them 45-27. They almost viewed it as a moral victory because they were expecting to get completely blown out.

BEDLAM THRILLER

The 1988 Bedlam game, which OU won 31-28, is known for an infamous late-game penalty and a dropped pass that would have won the game for us. In hindsight, I wish it could be remembered because of an onside kick.

We had a tough time stopping each other. Mike Gaddis and Barry Sanders ran up and down the field. Both finished with more than 200 rushing yards. When OU jumped out 14-0 on us, Sooner radio play-by-play man John Brooks said ESPN was looking for a replacement game to broadcast, but I still tease John that it turned out to be a better game than that.

We scored to go up 28-24 with 8:45 left. I never really second-guessed much of what we did tactically, but maybe I do second-guess myself about this game. We had considered using a surprise onside kick, and I wish I had pulled the trigger on it.

They were probably going to score anyway, so if they got the ball at midfield, so what? Maybe they would score a little quicker and we'd get the ball back with a decent amount of time left.

I didn't call for the onside kick because we bowed up defensively in the second half. We kicked off and they drove down to take a 31-28 lead.

We ripped right back downfield and our home crowd went bonkers. I didn't think they were going to stop us. But a yellow flag did.

PIVOTAL PENALTY

We ran an option play in front of OU's bench and Sanders was chased out of bounds. It was going to be fourth-and-inches at OU's 19.

A late penalty flag came sailing out. Our fullback, Garrett Limbrick, had gotten into a verbal exchange with OU linebacker Richard Dillon. I saw the flag come out from the opposite sideline and immediately thought, "This ain't good." I was talking to my coaches on the headset trying to see if they knew what was going on. Larry Coker said he thought they had called some kind of dead ball foul on Limbrick.

I asked the officials for a clarification. I know the guy who made the call. He's an NFL official. He's a good guy. The officials told me our guy had cussed them. It was just some pushing, not a confrontation. But we could see the OU guys lobbying to get the call when it happened. I don't blame them. We would have done the same thing.

I never was a guy to complain about officiating. But to this day, I don't think the situation merited a penalty. I can't say it was a bad call. Something was said over there. But at that particular point, I don't think you make a call that decides the game.

I said then and still maintain that Limbrick was not a hothead. We had some guys who were very good candidates for a personal foul, but neither he nor Richard Dillon was one of them. You just shouldn't make that call with 56 seconds left.

THE DROP

We still had one last chance to pull out a win.

The penalty gave us a fourth-and-16 at the OU 34. I told Larry Coker I wanted us to fire a pass down to the end zone.

Gundy ran around, we threw the tip drill, and it was executed perfectly. I saw the ball go up. It was a little hazy from the sideline as it went through an OU kid's hands. I couldn't tell exactly what happened with our receiver, Brent Parker, but I saw the cheerleaders fall down and their body language told me all I needed to know.

Brent got his hands on the ball, but he wasn't able to come down with it. He came by me and I said something to the effect of, "Get your head up and don't worry about it. Let's go." Brent wasn't Hart Lee Dykes, but he was a sure-handed guy. If I'd have had my druthers, Dykes would have had his hands on it. But Brent got in behind their defender and the ball went clean through OU's hands. Oklahoma ran the clock out. Game over.

SANDERS THE FRONTRUNNER

Barry Sanders ran for the second-most yards ever (215) against Oklahoma and jumped past Troy Aikman for first place in the Scripps-Howard Heisman poll.

Barry Switzer helped Sanders' candidacy because he told the media that Sanders was the best back in the country.

People can think what they may about Switzer, but I never had a problem with him. I thought part of his being Barry Switzer was that he was going to say what was on his mind. He wasn't dogging Oklahoma State or Barry Sanders or anything. He was very, very up front, and to this day says Sanders is the best back he's ever seen.

Meanwhile, Sanders told reporters after the Bedlam game that he wished he didn't have to talk about the Heisman race and he wished football was only a team sport. It wasn't false humility. He genuinely felt that way. That's why he began changing clothes and getting out of the dressing room quickly after games. He literally did not take showers so he could leave before the locker room was opened to the media.

Of course, Sanders needed to be available to the media if we were going to generate Heisman publicity for him. Steve Buzzard handled things like a pro, particularly when attention started mounting. Sanders received a lot of requests from the national media and, as little as he liked doing it, did his part.

ANGER MANAGEMENT

I had two sources of irritation the week after the Bedlam game. One was a poor defensive performance against Kansas and the other was a meeting with the NCAA Infractions Committee.

We beat Kansas 63-24, but they accumulated 356 yards by halftime and my patience with the defense was wearing thin. The Jayhawks couldn't stop Sanders and he ran for 312 yards, his third 300-yard rushing game of the season. We overcame our defensive issues by hanging 717 yards on Kansas.

Immediately after the game, I had to get on a jet and fly to Tucson, Arizona, to see the Infractions Committee. Mike Glazier and Mike Slive, our attorneys, started prepping me for the meeting. I didn't want to go, but I had to, so I sat there saying, "Yes sir," or "No sir," for half a day, or however long it was.

BACK TO BASICS

We were all getting frustrated with what was happening on defense, so at some point late in the season I told Louis Campbell and our defensive coaches that we were going to cut back on what we were doing and just use base plays. I don't think our defensive issues were anybody's fault. We knew we were going to

Our hotel was a nice place and the food was OK, but our workout facility was an old baseball park with Astroturf and dirt basepaths. It was not what I would call a real good workout facility.

A couple of nights before the game, they had a reception for Tech and us in the Tokyo Dome. Guys were assigned to serve as our interpreters, and sometimes they would act like they couldn't understand us even when we knew they could. We needed to communicate with them when we got to the reception and saw that there were big vats and cases of beer and rice wine on the players' tables. I told our interpreters that we had to get the booze out of there, so they scurried around to get it done.

We had a crew of Southwest Conference officials with us. They were good guys, some of whom I knew from my old Southwest Conference days. But somebody told me to make sure I stayed on top of the folks staging the game because they weren't familiar with our version of football.

The first time we went to the Tokyo Dome, I asked where they were going to put our coaches. They weren't going to put them in a press box. They were going to put them up in the stands, like in row 28. I told them it wasn't going to be that way and we had to have a box. Our administrative assistant, Marty Sargent, did a yeoman's job clearing some of this up. Our coaches used some kind of makeshift press box during the game. But there were plenty of things like this to worry about, and the referee never could find the 30-second play clock.

WAKE-UP CALL

Sanders had to miss the Heisman Trophy presentation because our game in Tokyo was scheduled the same day as the Heisman ceremony in New York. His parents and his brother, who was a heck of a running back at Northwestern University, went to New York on Barry's behalf.

The TV folks wanted to get some kind of reaction from Sanders when the announcement was made. The original plan was just to set up some cameras and lights in our hotel lobby. Because of the time difference from Tokyo to New York, we were going to have to do it at something like 4 a.m., but we figured we could wake Barry up at the last minute and make the best of it.

Well, our sports information director, Steve Buzzard, came up to me. He knew I was going to erupt, but he said we couldn't do the TV business in the hotel lobby because of satellites or something. They wanted to know if we could do it at a TV studio in downtown Tokyo.

I didn't like that idea at all because our game was later that day and I didn't want to wake Sanders up that early to drive him around. He was not going to want to do it, and I didn't feel like asking him. I said I would go to the TV studio, but I was not going to bother Sanders and bring him down there. I told that to our athletic director, Myron Roderick, and he understood.

Myron told the TV people, but they raised cain. Myron came back and asked me to figure out some way to get Sanders down there.

Buzzard, Shimek, or somebody came up with the idea of inviting the offensive linemen and our fullback, Garrett Limbrick, to the TV studio to help entice Sanders to come along. I told the linemen that we needed their help. They were all excited, including Limbrick, and they were going to make sure Sanders got up and went with us.

I told Myron he had to get more limos because we weren't going to throw all those folks, especially the big linemen, in a cab. I said, "Go get however many limos it will take for them all to ride comfortably."

Sanders was alright about the deal. He never said he wasn't going to do it. He just didn't want to get up. But we got all of our guys in limos and we were driving through downtown Tokyo going God knows where.

We pulled up to a high rise where the CBS affiliate in Tokyo is located. Those linemen, they were digging it. I had told the TV people that they had better have a bunch of food there for our guys, so they had coffee, donuts, and breakfast stuff waiting for them.

We wanted to get in and out of there in a hurry because kickoff was only about seven hours later and we still had to take care of all of our pregame planning. They told me that Barry and I were going to be in a little studio by ourselves, the Heisman people would make the announcement, and Sanders would say a few words on live television if he won. I told them we couldn't hang around for interviews, and they swore to me we wouldn't have to do any.

Well, they made the announcement that Sanders had won it and they turned the camera on us. From what I remember, Barry thanked them and said he felt honored to accept the award for his school. I then heard Bob Costas, who was on the broadcast crew in New York, tell viewers, "Stay right here and we'll be right back with an interview of Barry Sanders." And that was after I had been promised we wouldn't have to stick around.

I was really irritated and didn't know what to do, but there were some plugs in the wall, so I just reached down, pulled out the plugs, and we got out of there.

Years later, when I was with the Miami Dolphins, I apologized to Costas. He remembered me pulling the plug on things.

JUST GETTING STARTED

It was a big deal for us to be in Japan, and it was a big deal for them to have a Heisman Trophy winner present.

When we went out for pregame warmups, it seemed like everybody in Japan had a camera. We didn't know whether they were media people or not, but we had to shoo them out of our drills. We had been doing the same thing at practices. Otherwise, they would all be right out there among us.

We had to run off a whole ocean of guys with cameras when we took the field for warm-ups. We didn't speak Japanese, but we finally determined we could speak a universal language to get our point across.

Meanwhile, the referee tells me he still can't find the 30-second clock. But this is just one of many distractions.

Our dressing room was big and nice because it was a brand-new stadium, but they just had folding chairs around the walls and no lockers.

We were milling around waiting for the game to start, and I could see there was some kind of commotion in the room.

I asked what was going on and was told that the Miami Dolphins cheerleaders were in a dressing room right next to ours with nothing in front of the door. Our guys did what you would expect college males to do. Some of them were trying to check out the view.

I was so mad about it that I didn't take a peek. We raised hell and somebody got us some stuff to tape over the door so our players could concentrate on the Red Raiders instead of female anatomy. It was tough to set a tone to win a football game with everything going on around us.

I was usually considerate enough to ask our liaison if there was anything I needed to do and he always told me no. But he came up with an unwanted surprise before the game. He said he needed Sanders and me on the field immediately for some kind of presentation with Mike Mansfield, a former senator who was U.S. ambassador to Japan.

I didn't want to be rude because they had no comprehension of our protocol, but I didn't want to take Sanders out there. We were getting ready to play a football game.

I found a pinch-hitter in our university president, Dr. John Campbell. I asked him if he would stand in for Sanders and me at the ceremony. Dr. Campbell was a good guy and was glad to do it, so he went out there and accepted a nice gift—some kind of samurai head or something—on our behalf. Dr. Campbell saved us. If he had said no, I don't know what we would have done. I probably would have made somebody else mad. I was ready to get on with the game.

ASSAULTING OUR EARS

Texas Tech quarterback Billy Joe Tolliver led the Southwest Conference in total offense that season and we couldn't stop him. He threw for 446 yards, which was a school record.

The Japanese crowd didn't understand the game, but they had been given noisemakers and little drums and everything. Every time somebody threw the ball, they cheered, whether it was completed or not, so you can imagine how many times they cheered considering the number of passes Tolliver fired.

There were no acoustics in the building. It was incredibly noisy and the Grambling band was right there next to our bench. Because of the loudness quotient, my head was splitting.

The noise actually worked in our favor once. We were going to call a fake punt. Garrett Limbrick was the upback and he was supposed to yell some trigger word that would call off the fake if they lined up a certain way. Limbrick was trying to yell the trigger word, but the dome was so loud that hardly anybody could hear it. The center snapped the ball and it wedged in the armpit of Limbrick, who didn't know the ball was coming. Limbrick took off and ran for a first down. We pulled out all the stops because we needed to win the game.

Sanders ran for nearly a mile and we got just enough stops for a 45-42 victory.

CHAOS CONTINUES

We got popped with another surprise after the game. They wanted us to walk to the opposite side of the arena through a crowd of people for a postgame press conference. We didn't have an escort or anything to get us past the mob.

I balked and told them we were going to our dressing room and to send the media over if they wanted anything.

There must have been a jillion people and 90 million cameras in that small room and I was battling a headache because of everything that had gone on. I did my postgame talk, Sanders said just a few words, and the interpreters translated it all.

When we left the room, they all rushed out with us to take more pictures of Sanders. I felt sorry for Spike and Billy Joe. They were standing there and nobody wanted to talk to them.

Rick Telander was there for *Sports Illustrated* and I invited him to ride with us on the bus after the game. He sat in my seat and I told him how exhausted we were. You talk about a full day. I don't know how we survived it, let alone won the game.

STAYING BUSY

It seemed like it took forever to fly back to Dallas. We bused back to Stillwater and were all beat. I was not pleased to hear that someone had arranged a "Welcome Back" celebration for Sanders in Stillwater. They had set up a stage on the practice field next to Gallagher-Iba Arena and we had to get directly off the bus to go to it.

We walked through the crowd and I introduced poor Barry, who just wanted to go home. I wanted to go home, too. We said a few things and thanked the crowd. Somebody said something about an autograph session. I cussed and said, "We are not doing that."

The sports information staff didn't set up the welcome back event. It was set up by the university, so I was getting more irritated at some folks in our administration. It was building to a point that they didn't seem to have any regard for Barry.

Barry Sanders, a Heisman Trophy winner and Pro Football Hall of Famer, had perhaps the greatest season by a player in college football history in 1988. *Photo courtesy of Oklahoma State University*

BIG APPLE BARRY

We didn't have any time to recover from Japan. We were scheduled to leave for New York the next day so Sanders could be honored as the Heisman Trophy winner.

Bill Shimek and I accompanied Barry on the trip and we flew up with Sanders' family members, who met us in St. Louis. I remember at the time that William Sanders, Barry's father, was strongly suggesting his son was not going to leave school early for the NFL.

We went to a private function at the Downtown Athletic Club for Barry and former Heisman winners. It was a classic room with paneled walls and portraits of all the recipients. Those guys took turns up there talking about what it meant to be a Heisman winner and we were just in awe.

The magnitude of what it means to win the Heisman finally struck Sanders when Earl Campbell came over and asked Barry to sign two programs. After Earl walked away with the signatures, Barry looked at me and said, "Coach, do you realize who that was? Earl Campbell just asked for my autograph." I reminded him that he was a Heisman winner and I told him to look around the room. He didn't know who Hopalong Cassady or Vic Janowicz was, but the scope of this honor was finally dawning on him.

We went to the Marriott Marquis for a huge banquet the next evening. It was the second-largest crowd I had ever spoken to, behind the Texas high school coaches' clinic. I remember trying to smooth things over since Barry had said winning the Heisman wasn't a big deal. He didn't mean anything negative by that. He was a legitimately good guy from a great family. It's not that they didn't think the Heisman was important. They were just very humble people. And Barry got up there and did a great job.

They gave us two Heismans in a little holding room. One was for Barry's family and the other was for Oklahoma State. We wanted to take the university's trophy back with us to use during a recruiting weekend.

The Heisman is a heavy trophy, but Bill Shimek carried that thing under his arm through LaGuardia Airport. This was before the massive security used at airports nowadays.

It seems like we had an extra seat, and Bill just belted the Heisman down next to him in the front of the plane. Heads were turning and Bill, who has such an incredibly dry sense of humor, told people who did double takes that this was the senior Heisman Trophy and he was the senior Heisman winner or something like that.

SAN DIEGO OR BUST

A lot of bowls tried to make deals with us long before the regular season was over because of our star power. We were not going to get to go to one of the big New Year's Day bowls, but we wanted the next most prestigious bowl and a good trip for our players. We accepted a bid to the Holiday Bowl in San Diego, but few people know that we almost didn't go to any bowl.

Nobody self-imposed penalties on themselves for NCAA violations during this time, but our attorneys proposed that we take ourselves out of a bowl game since it might make the NCAA go easier on us. It would have been a groundbreaking gesture had we decided to do it.

Our athletic director, president, and head of the board of regents told me it was my call and that they would support whatever decision I made. I told them I couldn't stand in front of this squad and tell them they weren't going to a bowl game. If this had been a seven-win or eight-win team heading to the Bluebonnet Bowl, I probably wouldn't have any qualms about staying home, but we had the Heisman Trophy winner and a chance to win 10 games. That team deserved to go to a bowl.

Nobody ever brought it up to me again, even when the NCAA handed us a severe penalty.

HOTEL CALIFORNIA

While jockeying for bowl bids, I told the Holiday Bowl people we would accept their invitation if they could guarantee we would stay at the Hyatt Regency Islandia on Mission Bay. I loved that area because it was easy to get around, and it had Sea

World and boat docks. I also loved it because I could jog around Mission Bay and La Jolla was right up the road.

The organizers were ecstatic to have a Heisman Trophy winner. I don't know that they ever had one before then. We were hoping to play somebody with better credentials than Wyoming, but they had only lost one regular-season game and were picked to be our opponent.

I flew out for a pregame function, and the highlight for me was sitting at a table with Sid Gillman. He was a pass guru, but he told me he had seen our tailback and could understand why we would run the ball.

We also had one of those joint team functions with Wyoming. I took Gundy, Sanders, and Dykes. They took their good quarterback, Randy Welniak, a running back from Wichita named Dabby Dawson, and Pat Rabold, a defensive tackle and the WAC's defensive player of the year.

It struck me that Dykes was way bigger than the WAC defensive player of the year. Even though Sanders and Gundy weren't large, our three guys were damn good-looking athletes. I knew who was going to win the ball game.

GETTING DEFENSIVE

It made the other defensive coaches mad because they thought I was shoving stuff down their throats, but Brent Guy and I made up the defensive game plan. Houston had a good player named Lamar Lathon and they gave Wyoming trouble that season, so we copied a version of what they did and found out Wyoming still didn't have any answers for it.

Wyoming scored a bunch of points that season, but we ran a strain of the same blitz repeatedly and sacked them seven times. Sim Drain and Stacey Satterwhite both played well and we held the team to 204 yards and 14 first downs. Statistically, it was easily our best defensive game that season.

All of our big guns on offense put up great numbers and we beat Wyoming 62-14. We probably could have scored 100, but we called off the dogs and I later teased their coach, Paul Roach, that I had got back at him for that "Welcome, Oklahoma" hotel sign which greeted us in Laramie the year before.

END OF AN ERA

I felt good as I was walking out of Jack Murphy Stadium after the game. We had won by a big margin and had 10 victories for the second year in a row.

Standing beside one of the pillars at the stadium was William Sanders, Barry's father. I had a good idea of what he was going to tell me, but I asked him what was on his mind. He told me Barry was ready to leave school a year early and enter the NFL draft.

I told William we would get together later and do whatever the family wanted to make sure everything was handled properly. Then I got on the bus, rode back, and had a great evening in Mission Bay.

While in the NFL, every time I went to Jack Murphy Stadium I showed guys that pillar and told them that story.

That moment really sums up this whole era. I know we were fixing to face a huge hit by the NCAA. I didn't know how big, but I knew it was going to be substantial. And I was the last guy to walk out of Jack Murphy Stadium when the curtain all of a sudden came down on this "lightning in a bottle" period.

It hit me immediately that the most exciting 10 years of football in Oklahoma State history had run their course and we were all moving on to another phase of life. But we were all fortunate to have been a part of what had just taken place.

CHAPTER 13

Final Thoughts

THE VERDICT ARRIVES

We got our bad news from the NCAA shortly after the 1988 season ended. We held a press conference the first week of January in 1989 to give everyone the details. We were placed on a four-year probation, including a three-year bowl ban and a two-year television ban. We also were stripped of 15 scholarships over a three-year period.

I stood at the front of that press conference and said, "If you want to blame anyone, blame me, because I am the head coach." Too many good people were hurt. Some very good alumni were used and some of them were ordered to disassociate from the program. Each of the individuals had been abused. They weren't criminal folks and, after the fact, I knew they had been taken advantage of—I hated that part of it.

Make no mistake about it. The sanctions handed to us were severe. You have to go back to the SMU death penalty enforcement to find a more devastating punishment for a football program. Not many people know this, but we could have been hit even harder than we were.

In addition to everything else, the NCAA's original recommendation was to ban us from playing any non-conference games or home games in 1989. We would have played a seven-game conference schedule on the road, and that's it. This was going to be a limited version of the death penalty.

What would that have done to the Stillwater economy? What would that have done to our budget?

I thought about the situation again when the NCAA told Baylor it couldn't play any non-conference basketball games during the 2005-2006 season. We avoided having to go through what Baylor went through because the NCAA cut us some slack for being cooperative. Another reason we were given the benefit of the doubt was because of the good work done by our attorneys, Mike Glazier and Mike Slive.

CLEANING THINGS UP

When we left the Infractions Committee meeting, they read off a list of the years we had previously been in front of them and they asked, "What do we have to do to keep you from coming back again?" We suffered for the past transgressions at Oklahoma State and that was spelled out to us.

When this stuff occurred under my watch, I thought they might fire me and I didn't care if they did. But I knew something had to be done to keep the program out of the NCAA doghouse. That was not the way to try to win games. I don't mean to sound holier than thou, because I'll get in a knife fight myself if I have to—at least figuratively. But things just couldn't be this way when rules were being broken every few years. It was a vicious cycle and it had to change.

I think the facilities Boone Pickens and Mike Holder are building over in Stillwater will help eliminate these kinds of issues. Mr. Pickens made the biggest donation in the history of college athletics and donors like Sherman Smith have also chipped in to help Oklahoma State build some of the finest facilities in the country. If you have great facilities, it allows you to be competitive in recruiting and, traditionally, the facilities had been lacking.

TAKING ONE FOR THE TEAM

We went from winning 10 games a year to losing 10 games a year in a three-season span. It was hard work digging out of probation, but it didn't eat me alive and I stayed for six seasons after the probation was handed down.

Our coaches were paid to put up with what we went through. A lot of them took advantage of opportunities to move on to better conditions and I didn't blame them.

The guys who I think suffered the most during the probationary period were the players. Any one of them could have transferred immediately to another school in 1989 and not lost any eligibility. I still remember that Ken Hatfield called and tried to bamboozle me into letting Stacey Satterwhite play at Arkansas. But not one of those kids transferred, and that still means a lot to me. It was an immense show of loyalty.

I felt sorry for what those players had to endure. They never had another winning season and had to play at places like Ohio State, Florida, and Michigan over the next few years, fighting through an 0-10-1 season.

If there's ever a group that Oklahoma State owes a lot to, it's Stacey Satterwhite, Mike Clark, Rod Smith, and the guys who endured such stuff when we were so short-handed on the field. To this day, I have so much respect for them and am sorry they had to put up with it.

We eventually dug out of probation to some degree. But on the same hand, it took a toll on all of us and it beat me up pretty good.

Many Oklahoma State assistant coaches later made a mark as college head coaches or in the NFL, including Houston Nutt (left) and Kevin Steele (middle). *Photo courtesy of Oklahoma State University*

TWO STRIKES

We suffered a double whammy after the 1988 season because we got rocked by probation and lost our Heisman Trophy winner to the NFL a year early.

I think Sanders would have left early even if we hadn't gone on probation, but I still wonder what would have happened if we had treated him differently. Everybody wanted a piece of the kid and every Posse Club wanted him to speak. What if we had told him we were going to shield him from people who wanted to pull him in 100 different directions? What if all he had to do at Oklahoma State was go to class and play football?

He could have stayed. I wouldn't bet my life on it, but it could have happened.

I felt sorry for the kid, because he was pestered to death about whether he was going to go to the NFL.

Barry's mother, Shirley, was an unbelievable lady and she didn't want Barry to leave school. William changed his mind during the course of things because a lot of pressure was put on his son to come out early. It was all handled well, so I didn't have any problem with that. Barry's workout for NFL teams was legendary and he got drafted by the Detroit Lions—their coach, Wayne Fontes, lit a cigar after watching Barry work out. The kid became arguably the best running back ever to play the game, so you can't second-guess his decision.

PARTING SHOT

I left Oklahoma State following the 1994 season and coached in the NFL for more than a decade with the Miami Dolphins and Oakland Raiders. Because I spent 16 seasons at OSU, I think I am qualified to make this statement: The long-term future of

FINAL THOUGHTS

Oklahoma State football seems to be in good hands and I think the program's best days are ahead, thanks to people like Boone Pickens and Sherman Smith and Mike Gundy. Enjoy the ride. I enjoyed mine.

Index

A

ABC 86, 88
Aikman, Troy 74, 117, 159, 161
Anderson, Ernest v, 23, 32, 36, 39, 40, 41, 43, 51, 57, 63, 72, 73
Anderson, Willie 46, 47, 48, 69, 72, 73, 120
Ankerson, Colin 18, 26
Antle, Rick 7, 12, 18, 20
Archer, David 61
Arizona State University v, 5, 47, 70, 71, 74, 75, 76, 77
Arkansas State University 69
Arkansas Tech University 2
Army 115
Auburn University 120, 154

B

Bailey, David 161
Bailey, Harold 7, 11, 18
Barr, Johnny 120
Baylor University 3, 62, 63, 70, 175
Best, Rob 108
Bicknell, Jack 125, 126
Bird, Larry 141
Boger, Larry 10
Boisvert, John 153
Boone, Curtis 7
Boston Bruins 85
Boston College 107, 125
Bosworth, Brian 117
Bowden, Bobby 111, 113
Bowling Green State University 77
Bozik, Ed 106, 107, 108, 109, 110
Bradley, Phil 15
Bradshaw, Terry 5
Brant, Tim 79
Brigham Young University 83
Brooks, John 157
Brown, Mack 61
Brown, Rod v, 41, 77, 90
Brown, Vernon 118, 119, 132
Brown, Watson 61
Broyles, Frank 62, 79, 84, 85
Bryant, Bear 81, 96
Buffalo Bills 73, 141, 142
Burns, Keith 149
Buzzard, Steve 147, 154, 160, 164

C

Cameron University 5
Campbell, Earl 73, 170
Campbell, John 166, 167
Campbell, Louis 96, 113, 114, 115, 117, 160
Campbell, Mel 18
Cardriche, Jaime 131
Carlson, Cody 63

INDEX

Casillas, Tony 107
Cassady, Hopalong 170
CBS 145, 165
Chachere, Gary 31
Chambers, Todd 91
Chesley, John 21, 33
Cincinnati Reds 51
Clark, James 98, 99
Clark, Ken 156
Clark, Mike 149, 176
Clayton, Mark 40
Clemson University 47
Cleveland Browns 24
Coker, Larry 46, 67, 79, 89, 97, 117, 124, 132, 158, 159
Colbert, Brandon 152
Connors, Bill v, vi, 133
Cook, Kelly 51
Cooper, John 46, 64, 78
Corker, John v, 7, 11
Costas, Bob 165
Couch, Cary 121
Crawford, Charles 76, 82
Criner, Jim 105
Crutchfield, Dwayne 33
Culp, Curley 47
Cummings, Torrance 161
Curry, Bill 150

D

Dabbs, Ken 72, 73
Dallas Cowboys 1
Davis, Butch 5, 37, 67, 69, 70, 72, 73
Davis, Dirk 28, 29
Dawson, Dabby 172
Deckard, Jerry 126
Dennis, Brad 98, 105
Denver Broncos 106
Detroit Lions 178
Dickerson, Eric 40, 73
Dickey, Jim 41, 46, 103
DiClementi, Pete 7, 11, 31
Dillard, Andy 85
Dillard, J.R. 130, 138, 139, 146
Dillon, Richard 158, 159
Dixon, Rickey 139
Dockery, John 145
Doerner, John 15, 21, 22, 23, 29, 32
Dooley, Vince 51
Drain, Sim 146, 149, 172

Drake University 130
Drake, Charlie 65
Dupree, Marcus 41, 57
Dykes, Hart Lee v, 74, 91, 92, 111, 113, 117, 122, 124, 125, 127, 135, 137, 138, 142, 145, 146, 153, 155, 157, 159, 172
Dykes, Spike 162, 168

E

Eben, Hermann 127
Endicott, Steve 8
ESPN 83, 105, 106, 127
Essington, Randy 40

F

Fair, Jeff 121
Faulks, Frank 45
Fazio, Foge 106, 110
Ferguson, Chip 113
Fisher, Roderick 21, 24, 31
Florida State University 33, 34, 107, 111, 113
Flutie, Doug 125, 126
Fontes, Wayne 178
Foote, Tad 65
Foster, Melvin 120
Freeman, Doug 7
Fry, Hayden 2
Fry, Joel 118, 119
Fryar, Irving 52, 55
Fuller, Leon 2

G

Gaddis, Mike 157
Gage, Steve 78
Gaines, Rodderick 123, 124
Gibbs, Gary 57
Gildon, Jason 149
Gill, Turner 52, 55
Gilliam, Melvin 91, 134, 149
Gillman, Sid 172
Glazier, Mike 160, 175
Gottfried, Mike 110
Grambling State University 161, 167
Grant, Kenneth 130
Green, Hugh 10
Green, Jarrod 146
Green, Mike 31

Gundy, Cale 115
Gundy, Judy 115
Gundy, Mike 18, 74, 95, 114, 115, 117, 120, 123, 124, 125, 126, 135, 138, 142, 145, 146, 150, 151, 153, 159, 172, 179
Gundy, Ray 115
Guy, Brent 35, 172

H

Haden, Pat 145
Ham, James 50
Hamilton, Leonard 131
Hanna, Barry 89
Harding, Rodney 21, 31, 49, 50, 51, 58, 63, 76, 78, 88
Harris, Jamie 37, 52, 78, 85
Harris, Major 144, 145, 161
Harris, Terrel 83
Hatfield, Ken 62, 176
Hector, Johnny 34
Heinzler, Steve 7, 18
Helms, Jim 4, 5
Henderson, Tracy 59, 83
Herring, Reggie 33, 34, 37, 48, 59, 69, 120
Hilger, Rusty 32, 33, 37, 52, 63, 79, 81, 85, 95
Hill, Greg 129
Hinds, Adam 37, 39
Holder, Mike 175
Holieway, Jamelle 117, 139
Holton, Larry 3, 4, 5, 46
Holtz, Lou 62
Hudson, Gerald 114, 118
Hudson, Mike 55
Huff, Sam 88

I

Iba, Henry 65, 66, 90
Igo, Kevin 21
Illinois State University 126
Ingram, Ronald 11, 15
Iowa State University 18, 20, 26, 33, 43, 59, 62, 83, 104, 105, 111, 117, 118, 119, 126, 127, 141, 161

J

Jackson, Bo 154

Jackson, Ike 37, 39, 40, 63
Jackson, Keith 79
Jackson, Ricky 10
Jankovich, Sam 65
Janowicz, Vic 170
Jette, Paul 4, 5, 11, 47, 48, 51, 59, 67, 69, 95, 96, 107
Johnson, Gregg 7
Johnson, Jimmy v, 1, 2, 3, 4, 5, 6, 7, 8, 10, 11, 13, 14, 15, 16, 17, 18, 20, 21, 23, 27, 29, 32, 34, 36, 37, 40, 43, 45, 46, 47, 48, 50, 52, 54, 58, 59, 61, 62, 63, 64, 65, 66, 69, 70, 71, 76, 78, 107, 109
Johnson, Kim 130
Johnson, Linda Kay 1, 62
Johnson, Merv 132, 133
Johnson, Troy 139
Jones, Becky 27, 121
Jones, Devin 161
Jones, Hasan 113
Jones, Jean 1
Jones, Jerry 1, 13, 62
Jones, Shawn 29, 32, 51, 52, 78, 82
Jordan, Michael 141

K

Kansas City Chiefs 45, 129
Kansas State University 18, 32, 41, 46, 58, 59, 82, 103, 118, 119, 126, 138, 157
Keith, Brien 130
Kelly, Jim 134
Ketchum, Ed 67
Kidder, Jason 153
Krebs, Jim 48, 50, 77, 103
Kubiak, Gary 34

L

Lacewell, Larry 69, 70
Lashar, Tim 56
Lathon, Lamar 172
Leahy, Bob 4, 5, 7, 13, 14, 15, 18, 24, 32, 33, 36, 43, 46
Leonard, Kevin 1, 66, 67
Lewis, Bill 47
Lewis, Darren 152
Lewis, Gary v, 31
Lewis, Malcolm 85
Limbrick, Garrett 158, 164, 167
Lincoln Journal Star 129

INDEX 183

Long, Howie 27
Luper, Curtis 73, 74

M

Mackey, Shawn 146
MacPherson, Dick 70
Maguire, Paul 106
Malcolm and Eddie 131
Manley, Dexter 7, 8, 10, 11, 12, 148, 149
Mansfield, Mike 166
Marino, Dan 95
Maritan, Doug 28, 29
Marshall, Bo 14
Martin, Dan 14
McClintock, John 84, 85
McDowell, Gene 34
Meacham, Doug 138
Miami Dolphins 39, 40, 62, 125, 161, 165, 166, 178
Miami University 100, 150, 152
Michigan State University 75
Miller, Bernie 78
Miller, Bill 5
Miller, Joe 49
Miller, Terrance 118, 119
Mitchell, Brian 122
Monger, Matt 48
Moon, Lee 103
Moore, Jerry 108
Moore, Mark v, 55, 59, 61, 77, 97, 117, 124, 126
Morris, Bam 129
Morrison, Joe 2, 86, 88
Musburger, Brent 145

N

Nash, Mitch 132, 133
Nehlen, Don 145
New England Patriots 92
New Mexico State University 70
New York Giants 86, 88
Norseth, Mike 102
North Texas State University 2, 11, 26, 29, 31, 39, 51, 54, 56, 98
Northwestern University 163
Nutt, Houston 23, 69, 70, 124, 176

O

O'Neal, Leonard 37

O'Neal, Leslie v, 37, 49, 50, 51, 55, 76, 83, 90, 99, 102, 107, 111
Oakland Raiders 106, 178
Ohio State University 176
Oliver, Ruben 145
Osborne, Tom 156
Overstreet, David 47

P

Pardee, Jack 134
Parker, Brent 159
Parrish, Stan 157
Patrick, Mike 106
Pearson, Barry 4, 5
Peckman, Bill 106, 107
Peete, Rodney 161
Pennsylvania State University 51, 110
Perkins, Carl 29
Phillips University 91
Pickens, Boone 175, 179
Pickett, Dan 140
Pittsburgh Steelers 129
Pope, Kenith 130
Posvar, Wesley 108, 109
Prater, Dean 7, 24
Principia College 37, 39

Q

Quinn, Pat v, 86

R

Rabold, Pat 172
Rader, David 154
Rankin, Rusty 97
Raynor, Bobby 152
Rice University 61, 62
Richardson, Reggie 7
Riley, Bobby 85, 97, 122, 127
Ripley, Mickey 132, 133
Roach, Larry v, 29, 31, 58
Roach, Paul 135, 173
Robbins, Joyce 97
Roberts, Harry 58, 100, 104
Rockins, Chris 21, 24, 26, 31, 55, 56, 74
Roderick, Myron 58, 61, 66, 67, 69, 107, 108, 135, 164
Rogers, Darryl 70, 75, 76
Rogers, George 14
Rose, Pete 51

Rozier, Mike 52, 55
Rubley, T.J. 133
Ruth, Mike 107

S

San Diego Chargers 13
San Diego State University 23, 24, 29, 34, 43, 77, 78
Sanders, Barry v, 46, 74, 102, 111, 114, 118, 119, 120, 122, 123, 126, 132, 133, 134, 135, 138, 139, 140, 141, 145, 146, 147, 148, 150, 152, 153, 154, 155, 157, 158, 159, 160, 161, 162, 163, 164, 165, 166, 167, 168, 169, 170, 172, 173, 178
Sanders, Shirley 178
Sanders, William 170, 173, 178
Sargent, Marty 163
Satterwhite, Stacey 149, 172, 176
Schnellenberger, Howard 64
Seely, Brad 71, 76, 77, 105, 153
Sheffey, Darryl 18
Sheppard, T.G. 29
Sherrill, Jackie 2, 3, 5, 34, 52, 150, 152, 153
Shields, Will 129
Shimek, Bill 46, 47, 118, 119, 143, 144, 162, 164, 169, 170
Sims, Billy 47, 73
Singleton, Derek 32
Slive, Mike 160, 175
Slocum, R.C. 74
Smith, Larry 70
Smith, Neil 137
Smith, Rod 135, 149, 176
Smith, Rodney 12
Smith, Sherman 175, 179
Solomon, Bill 18
Southern Methodist University 8, 71, 78, 81, 96, 130, 174
Spencer, James 21
Sport 74
Sports Illustrated 43, 52, 54, 83, 95, 155, 168
Springer, Jim 98
Springer, Jim Jr. 98
Stanford University 118
Stanley, Chris 153
Stanley, Jim 1, 5, 46
Steele, Kevin 70, 120, 176

Steinkuhler, Dean 52, 153
Stokley, Nelson 122
Struthers, Jim 99
Stuckey, John 120
Suellentrop, Terry 15
Swann, Lynn 86
Swanson, Shane 81
Switzer, Barry 6, 16, 17, 85, 115, 117, 120, 143, 144, 159
Syracuse University 70, 71

T

Tampa Bay Buccaneers 15
Tarkenton, Fran 88
Taylor, Roger 12
Taylor, Steve 141
Taylor, Worley 7, 16, 18
Teaff, Grant 3
Telander, Rick 168
Texas A&M University 34, 52, 74, 129, 130, 150, 151, 152, 153
Texas Tech University 37, 52, 108, 129, 161, 162, 167
The New York Times 83
Thomas, Broderick 137
Thomas, Thurman v, 57, 72, 73, 74, 78, 82, 90, 95, 96, 97, 98, 100, 102, 103, 104, 105, 111, 112, 113, 117, 120, 121, 122, 124, 127, 131, 132, 133, 134, 135, 137, 138, 139, 140, 141, 142, 145, 146, 147, 148
Thompson, Warren 49
Tillman, Spencer 85
Tolliver, Billy Joe 167, 168
Tollner, Ted 45, 46
Traber, Jim 23, 26
Tramel, Jimmie v
Tulane University 45
Tulsa World v, 133

U

University of Alabama 81, 96, 150, 154
University of Arizona 70
University of Arkansas 2, 12, 13, 14, 16, 22, 23, 24, 34, 37, 48, 62, 71, 115, 176
University of California 5
University of California, Los Angeles 37, 143
University of Cincinnati 51

INDEX

University of Colorado 17, 18, 24, 31, 32, 34, 40, 57, 82, 102, 103, 126, 136, 154, 155
University of Florida 176
University of Georgia 43, 47, 51, 72
University of Houston 123, 124, 134, 172
University of Illinois 46
University of Iowa 120
University of Kansas 16, 23, 31, 40, 57, 81, 102, 118, 119, 126, 140, 160
University of Louisville 32, 40
University of Miami 46, 48, 50, 54, 64, 65, 69, 107
University of Michigan 83, 176
University of Missouri 15, 23, 32, 41, 54, 58, 83, 103, 104, 126, 127, 138, 157
University of Nebraska 15, 23, 32, 36, 41, 52, 54, 55, 56, 58, 59, 64, 78, 79, 81, 82, 100, 125, 126, 128, 129, 134, 136, 137, 141, 153, 155, 156
University of New Orleans 39
University of Notre Dame 150
University of Oklahoma 5, 6, 10, 15, 16, 17, 26, 27, 33, 41, 46, 47, 52, 55, 56, 57, 58, 61, 74, 83, 84, 85, 86, 91, 95, 104, 105, 107, 110, 115, 117, 118, 119, 120, 126, 127, 128, 130, 132, 133, 134, 139, 140, 143, 157, 158, 159, 173
University of Pacific 71
University of Pittsburgh 2, 3, 4, 5, 10, 52, 106, 107, 108, 109, 110, 111, 150, 152
University of South Carolina 2, 14, 86, 88, 89
University of Southern California 45, 96, 143, 146
University of Southwestern Louisiana 122, 136
University of Tennessee 46
University of Texas 2, 5, 61, 72, 73, 107
University of Tulsa 29, 39, 40, 46, 52, 64, 78, 100, 118, 119, 123, 133, 134, 154
University of Utah 149
University of Virginia 103
University of Washington 23, 95, 96, 97, 98, 113
University of Wisconsin 41
University of Wyoming 46, 134, 135, 172, 173
USA Today 91

Utah State University 35

V

Valesente, Bob 140
Van Raaphorst, Jeff 76
Verplank, Scott 85, 113
Verser, David 16
Villanova University 27
Vogel, Steve 31, 57, 82

W

Walden, Jim 141
Walker, Herschel 43
Walsh, Steve 161
Walstad, George 46, 67, 72, 98, 99, 100, 118, 119, 140, 144
Wannstedt, Dave 3, 4, 5, 14, 15, 27, 28, 36, 37, 45, 62
Wannstedt, Jan 27
War Pigs 153, 154
Ware, Andre 134
Warwick, Dionne 107
Washington Federals 64
Washington Redskins 8, 122
Washington, John 49, 50, 82
Wells, Billy 16
Wells, Kitty 29
Welniak, Randy 172
West Texas State University 21, 22
West Virginia University 100, 143, 144, 145, 146
White, Charles 96
Wichita State University 12
Wilder, James 15
Williams, Ronnie 81, 95, 96, 97, 100, 113, 122, 123, 124, 125, 135
Wilson, Tom 34
Wise, Tony 3, 4, 5, 39, 52, 70, 71
Wolfe, Mike 127, 153
Woodard, Byron 153

Y

Yancy, Windell 83
Young, Ricky v, 7, 31
Young, Terry 16

Z

Zachary, Ken 43, 81
Zentic, Mike 136

Celebrate the Heroes of Football
in These Other New and Recent Releases from Sports Publishing!

Football's Second Season: Scouting High School Game Breakers

ISBN-13: 978-1-59670-209-7
ISBN-10: 1-59670-209-5
$16.95 softcover

Tom Lemming wasn't college football's first "recruiting analyst," but he definitely perfected the role. He annually visits as many as 47 states and personally interviews the top 1,500 players in the country to produce the *Prep Football Report*. 2007 release!

Tales from the Sooners Sideline

ISBN-13: 978-1-59670-249-3
ISBN-10: 1-59670-249-4
$15.95 softcover

In this new softcover edition, dozens of stories look at the individual and team triumphs that commenced with the hiring of legendary coach Bud Wilkinson; the book also spans the careers of Barry Switzer and Bob Stoops and details seven national championships. 2007 release!

Game of My Life: Dallas Cowboys

ISBN: 1-59670-036-X
$24.95 hardcover

Players featured in this look at the most memorable games in Cowboys history include Roger Staubach, Tony Dorsett, Emmitt Smith, Randy White, Drew Pearson, Tony Hill, Deion Sanders, Chuck Howley, Larry Brown, and Bill Bates.

Captain Crash and the Dallas Cowboys

ISBN: 1-59670-103-X
$19.95 hardcover

In his second book, Dallas legend Cliff Harris gets up close and personal about his days as the hard-hitting free safety for America's Team in the 1970's, a decade that saw the Cowboys go to five Super Bowls and win two of them. This is a must-have for Cowboys fans.

The Oklahoma Football Encyclopedia

ISBN: 1-58261-699-X
$39.95 hardcover

This historical description of University of Oklahoma football from 1895 through 2005 shows how the team got its start and how head coach Bennie Owen laid the foundation for the Sooners to become one of college football's top programs.

Legends of the Dallas Cowboys

ISBN: 1-58261-707-4
$24.95 hardcover

This in-depth look at 15 of the legends that have shaped the Cowboys' identity begins with Coach Tom Landry, still the franchise's enduring image, and also includes Tex Schramm, Emmitt Smith, Roger Staubach, and Troy Aikman.

 All books are available in bookstores everywhere!
Order 24-hours-a-day by calling toll-free **1-877-424-BOOK (2665)**.
Also order online at **www.SportsPublishingLLC.com**.